1991

CHOOSING DEATH

The Park Ridge Center exists to explore the relationships among health, faith, and ethics. In its programs of research, publishing, and education, the Center gives special attention to the bearing of religious beliefs on questions that confront people as they search for health and encounter illness. It also seeks to contribute to ethical reflection on a wide range of health-related issues. In this work the Center collaborates with representatives from diverse cultures, religious communities, health care fields, and academic disciplines and disseminates its findings to people interested in health, religion, and ethics.

The Center is an independent, not-for-profit organization supported by subscribing members and by grants and gifts from foundations, corporations, and individuals. Additional information may be obtained by writing to the Park Ridge Center, 676 N. St. Clair, Suite 450, Chicago, IL 60611.

CHOOSING DEATH

Active Euthanasia, Religion, and the Public Debate

Edited by Ron P. Hamel

A book from the Park Ridge Center
for the Study of Health, Faith, and Ethics

Trinity Press International
Philadelphia

Trinity Press International
3725 Chestnut Street
Philadelphia, PA 19104

©1991 The Park Ridge Center
for the Study of Health, Faith, and Ethics

Typesetting: Micah Marty
Cover Design: Brian Preuss

Library of Congress Cataloging-in-Publication Data

Choosing death : active euthanasia, religion, and the public debate /
    Ron P. Hamel, editor.
        p. cm.
    "A book from the Park Ridge Center for the study of health,
faith, and ethics."
    Includes bibliographical references.
    ISBN 1-56338-031-5 (pbk.)

    1. Euthanasia—Moral and ethical aspects. 2. Euthanasia—
Religious aspects. 3. Euthanasia—Social aspects. I. Hamel, Ron P.,
1946– . II. Park Ridge Center (Ill.)

R726.c46 1991
179'.7—dc20
                                                    91-24448
                                                        CIP

Printed in the United States of America

92 93 94 95 96 97   7 6 5 4 3 2

CONTENTS

PREFACE

"There is a secret fear of the unknown 'perils of the soul,'" according to Carl Jung. At the deepest level of our being we are anxious about controlling the psychological and material forces that threaten our autonomy. This secret fear of unknown forces surfaced in the life of Janet Adkins as she faced the perils of Alzheimer's disease. The prospect of losing control so pained her that she sought out Dr. Jack Kevorkian and his "suicide machine." Was she right? Was she wrong? Were her actions justifiable?

Although there is debate about her course of action, Ms. Adkins's fear was understandable. The course of Alzheimer's disease is well documented. Physical and mental diminishment and death are inevitable. As Jung reminds us, "one should realize that this fear is by no means unjustifiable; on the contrary it is only too well founded." Fear of an unknown, uncontrollable future, as well as fear of a hopeless and painful present, is a powerful incentive for some to "end it all."

Today, the power of medicine to sustain life is often a source of fear rather than solace. As medical science continues to acquire dramatic new powers, the fullness of life not infrequently lapses intos states of mere biological existence. Although most people are not anxious to die, the majority have certain minimal expectations about an acceptable quality of life. The specter of minimal, even unconscious, existence is frightening. Death is recognized as inevitable, yet many people feel that others will unduly, even cruelly, delay the unavoidable. They do not wish to become victims of what they would consider useless or overly burdensome treatment.

Suddenly, the "perils of the soul" and our secret fears are associated with sustaining life rather than facing death. Paradoxically, continued life is now considered potentially perilous, while an easy death takes on the cloak of a constitutionally protected right. More and more people believe that direct action to end a human life can sometimes be moral. "To be or not to be" is no longer the musing of a solitary, troubled prince; it represents an authentic moral dilemma for reasonable people. The following report explains why active voluntary euthanasia, or direct killing, is emerging as a significant issue in our society.

The Park Ridge Center exists to explore the relationships among health, faith, and ethics. In its programs of research, publishing, and education the Center gives special attention to the bearing of religious beliefs on questions that confront people as they search for health and encounter illness. It also seeks to contribute to ethical reflection on a wide range of health-related issues. In this work the Center collaborates with representatives from diverse cultures, religious communities, health care fields, and academic disciplines.

As an interfaith, interdisciplinary, intercultural forum we are committed to working in the crosscurrents of competing ideas and worldviews. We believe this position allows us to remain open to diverse publics in a culturally and religiously pluralistic world. This report, aimed at both the general public and special audiences like hospital ethics committees, takes up the problems, issues, and concerns surrounding active euthanasia. The attitudes of religious traditions are an integral part of this presentation. We hope the report will serve as a helpful resource for the public policy debate that is now taking shape, nationally and internationally.

Laurence J. O'Connell, Ph.D., S.T.D.
President and CEO
The Park Ridge Center

CONTRIBUTORS

Albert W. Alschuler is the Wilson-Dickinson professor at the University of Chicago Law School.

James F. Bresnahan, S.J., J.D., L.L.M., Ph.D., is co-director of the Ethics and Human Values in Medicine Program at Northwestern University Medical School, Chicago, Illinois.

Ronald E. Cranford, M.D., is neurologist and medical ethicist at Hennepin County Medical Center, Minneapolis, Minnesota.

Edwin R. DuBose, Ph.D., is Associate for Theology, Ethics, and Clinical Practice at the Park Ridge Center.

Joseph Edelheit is rabbi at Temple Emmanuel, Chicago, Illinois.

Ron P. Hamel, Ph.D., is Senior Associate for Theology, Ethics, and Clinical Practice at the Park Ridge Center.

Albert R. Jonsen, Ph.D is professor of Ethics in Medicine, Department of Medical History and Ethics, University of Washington School of Medicine, Seattle.

Karen Lebacqz, Ph.D., is professor of Christian Ethics at the Pacific School of Religion, Berkeley, California.

Martin E. Marty, Ph.D., is Senior Scholar-in-Residence at the Park Ridge Center and editor of *Second Opinion*.

Robert Moss, M.D., is Director of Geriatrics, Department of Family Practice, Lutheran General Hospital, Park Ridge, Illinois.

Margaret Murphy, Ph.D., R.N., is Senior Staff Specialist of the National Commission on Nursing Implementation Project, Milwaukee, Wisconsin.

Ronald Otremba, M.D., is director of Hospice HealthEast at St. Joseph's Hospital, St. Paul, Minnesota.

Stephen Sapp, Ph.D., is a professor of religion at the University of Miami, Coral Gables, Florida.

Don C. Shaw is president of Hemlock of Illinois, Chicago.

Margaret Wolters, R.N., is program director of Hospice HealthEast at St. Joseph's Hospital, St. Paul, Minnesota.

1

Personal Narratives

Active voluntary euthanasia is not a theoretical question only. It arises in the daily struggles of many terminally ill and severely debilitated persons and their families. We begin this discussion of euthanasia with accounts of four people—one with AIDS, one with cancer, another with Alzheimer's disease, and one in a persistent vegetative state—in order to present the question of active voluntary euthanasia as it usually arises, namely, out of people's experiences. For many, because of their actual medical condition or because of the fear of a possible future medical condition, euthanasia becomes a very real option.

Case 1: Steve

A 32-year-old man diagnosed with acquired immunodeficiency syndrome (AIDS) two years previously, Steve took ziduvodine until its side effects of nausea, anemia, and especially a low white-blood-cell count required his removal from that regimen. Following an initial opportunistic infection with Pneumocystis carinii pneumonia (PCP), treatments with pentamidine provided him with periods of relatively good health until side effects again caused the cessation of the treatment. Hospitalized again, this time for pain in his extremities, he was diagnosed with cytomegalovirus (CMV), a viral infection that often afflicts people with immune deficiency. When discharged home, he continued to experience pain in his legs and feet, diarrhea, and occasional shortness of breath.

His family, pious Baptists from a small east Texas town, had difficulty accepting Steve's situation. At the time of Steve's diagnosis, his father had been dead for 10 years. Although his mother and brother had suspected his homosexuality, they denied it until confronted with this illness. His brother refuses to visit Steve. His mother is deeply hurt by her younger son's sexual orientation and is very upset that he has AIDS. She has shared her anger and grief with her pastor, who encourages her to pray for guidance and to work for Steve's deliverance from the abomination of homosexuality.

Steve attended Sunday school and church with his parents until his senior year in high school, when he began to break away from his parents and their expectations of him. It was during this period that he also began to wrestle with his ambivalent feelings toward homosexuality. Unable to talk with his parents, he confided in his pastor, who urged him to pray for forgiveness. To secure his pastor's approval, and to relieve a mounting emotional distress, Steve "renounced his temptation."

After moving to a large urban area, however, Steve gradually came to an acceptance of his homosexuality, although this acceptance involved distance from his parents and a rejection of his religious rearing. The process of acceptance involved a period of sexual experimentation. In 1986 he met Mark and fell deeply in love. They purchased a home and worked hard to make a life together. In his relationship with Mark, Steve came to be at peace with himself, finally accepting that his sexuality was not a sin. He recognized that he was a good man, warm and caring toward others, and that his life had meaning and value. He also discovered that spirituality and faith were important dimensions in his life. He believed, as one created in God's image, that he was privileged to work together with God to create his own life and identity.

Steve attended several churches—Methodist, Assembly of God, Roman Catholic, and Presbyterian—but was uncomfortable with their attitudes toward homosexuality. He was also upset at the claim made by some church leaders that AIDS is God's judgment on sinful gay men. With his own diagnosis,

Steve underwent a period of deep depression: he feared loss of physical control, abandonment, and death. With the support of his lover, Mark, various friends, and a volunteer support group, he came to an emotional acceptance of his condition. Through careful diet, exercise, attention to physician's orders, and involvement in community AIDS work, he regained a feeling of control over his life. As time passed, he also was able to find strength and comfort in his faith. Although he no longer attended church, he was able to give up any lingering bitterness about his religious upbringing.

Steve formed a deep attachment to the group of volunteers from a nearby congregation who assist Mark with homemaking services and with Steve's physical care. Suspicious at first of their motivation for helping (was he to be "delivered of his sins"?), he later began to talk with them about Christianity and his thoughts of death and a possible afterlife. He has concluded that one continues to exist even when one loses one's own body. This eternal life, according to Steve, is a state of being at one with God.

These thoughts, which enabled him to become reconciled with his anxieties and fears of death, created a desire for reconciliation with his family. His mother, however, still refuses to accept her son's homosexuality. She is convinced that if Steve renounces his homosexuality, "Jesus will heal" him of AIDS. She refuses to confront the reality of his declining condition, urging him to refuse painkillers so that he will not become a drug addict. The growing discomfort between his mother and Mark and the medical staff troubles Steve.

Hospitalized with another sudden, serious case of PCP, with persistent fever, fatigue, and shortness of breath on top of sudden, dramatic weight loss, Steve begins to feel that his illness has the upper hand. His vision is impaired due to CMV retinitis, and he is showing more serious indications of AIDS dementia complex, particularly periods of temporary confusion and loss of memory. While still competent—and at the urging of Mark, who is an oncologist—he has completed a living will specifying that no resuscitative efforts be made, including cardiopulmonary resuscitation, intubation, or the insertion of a tube for nutrition and hydration, if futile or marginally helpful. A copy of the living will has been given to his primary-care physician and placed in his medical record. Determined to fight as long as he can, Steve tries to maintain an optimistic outlook, although his phone calls to his family and friends have begun to take on a tone of finality.

Hoping to be discharged, Steve suddenly declares his desire to die at home, surrounded by the people who have come to mean so much to him. He does not want another hospitalization. After lengthy discussion, he and his lover feel comfortable with the decision, though Steve does not share his thoughts with his mother. She wants him to remain hospitalized, where everything can be done to prolong his life. Steve does not want his deteriorating condition to lead to what he perceives as a death without dignity; he wants his primary-care physician to assist his death with an overdose of medication. Recognizing that his physician may have qualms about complying with his request, Steve has asked Mark to help him when the time comes. He begins to plan for his funeral.

Extremely weak from his illness and in great pain, Steve remains in the hospital, bedridden and dependent upon his mother, Mark, and the staff for almost everything. As a result of his brain infection, he has weakness on his right side and an involuntary tremor. Chronic viral and protozoan infections in his bowel cause unrelenting diarrhea. He is incontinent, experiences extreme pain and vision problems, and receives a morphine drip with a push every two hours for the pain. Finally, Steve develops a cough and a fever. Having been through this before, Mark suspects that his lover is developing another lung infection. After tossing all night in discomfort, Steve tells Mark that he cannot take it anymore; it is time for him to die. He asks Mark to administer an overdose of morphine.

—*Edwin R. DuBose*

Case 2: Michael

Michael is a 53-year-old white, married male living with his wife in a small town in Minnesota. He was diagnosed in December 1989 with cancer of the lung and metastases to the brain. He had a series of radiation treatments, following a laminectomy (surgical removal of the posterior arch of a vertebra), in the same month.

Michael was born in a small northern Minnesota town. He was the middle child in a family of six siblings, three brothers and three sisters. When he was about 12 years old, his family moved to another small town, where he attended high school until the tenth grade. He went into the military, served in the Marines, and upon discharge, joined the National Guard. He worked for 14 years at a battery company, and after a strike he worked at various jobs until he finally took a job at a creamery, where he remained for 22 years. A baptized Catholic, he was a member of a local parish. His priest visited regularly, and a fellow parishioner brought communion twice a week to his home while he was ill.

His father died of leukemia about six years ago. His mother is currently suffering from depression, and this is difficult for Michael because she calls him often and tries to elicit information about his disease process and prognosis. Michael is a very quiet and private person. Keeping everything inside has been his manner of coping over the years.

His wife, Karen, is the primary caregiver, and the couple has five children. Karen is in good health, but she has a history of being treated for depression. She is currently on antidepressant medication. Michael and Karen have always handled the finances, written checks, and balanced the checkbook together. Finances are a grave concern for the couple: they have applied for Social Security disability but will not receive anything for six months. Michael wrote his own will, not feeling it necessary to employ a lawyer because their finances are relatively simple. He frequently expresses concern about how Karen will manage financially both during his illness and after his death.

Both Michael and Karen are angry and depressed about his prognosis and his health status. Karen often expresses anger toward her mother-in-law because of her inappropriate phone calls. Michael's mother is unable to understand his inability to communicate his feelings and continues to press him to talk about his cancer. Michael has had a difficult time dealing with loss and crisis in the past. His style was to "hang in there" long after most people would have given up. For example, he worked at a job for 22 years "hating every day." He also felt very "duty bound": it was his responsibility to provide financially for his family regardless of his job satisfaction.

Before his illness he enjoyed fishing, playing softball, and coaching boxing in the community.

His children are a support to him. Three children live close by and visit frequently. Two sons have a history of chemical abuse and have participated in a treatment program with positive results. Michael and Karen have protected their children from much involvement in Michael's dying. There are 10 grandchildren.

On April 20, 1990, Michael was admitted to a program of hospice care. He was experiencing much discomfort and pain from shingles, located on the left side of his trunk. The main issue at the time of admission was to find a degree of pain control so that he could enjoy some quality of life. He remained at home for about one month with his wife caring for him. During that time, the children visited on occasion. The family refused any volunteer respite care, and Karen remained constantly at his side. Pain and nausea continued to be distressing symptoms, at times unmanageable. Eight days after beginning the program, a tube for introducing or withdrawing fluid was inserted in the membrane surrounding his spinal cord; Michael could then receive morphine sulfate through this epidural catheter to achieve comfort. He responded well and was able to enjoy some days free of pain and nausea. His appetite was fair to poor, and he continued to lose weight. The local VFW rallied to the family's need by organizing a benefit in Michael's honor and raised $4,000. Although Michael planned to attend, he was unable to do so because of extreme pain. The following week he was feeling good, eating well, and had even attended National Guard maneuvers.

On the day following the maneuvers, Michael notified the hospice nurse that he was in excruciating pain. The morphine dose was increased, and Decadron was added. Michael responded well. A family care conference was conducted the next day in the patient's home to address concerns of the patient and family. During the conference Michael's pain escalated. His wife and children cried and expressed their love for him. Michael remained noncommunicative, indicating he was in too much pain to talk. When respite care at the hospital was suggested, he refused because he was afraid "he would never come home again." He frequently voiced his concerns about the "unfinished" business of the finances. His desire was to remain at home and die there with his family present. At the end of the conference Michael was in extreme pain, and his family questioned why something could not be done to relieve it. That evening Michael was admitted to the inpatient hospice unit for management and assessment of agonizing pain due to his metastatic carcinoma.

He had been receiving a number of painkillers and other drugs. His medical regimen included epidural morphine injections of 5 mg. an hour and also 10–20 mg. of Thorazine every six hours, 50 mg. of Elavil at bedtime, 3 mg. of Decadron four times per day, and 150 mg. of theophylline twice a day, along with 800 mg. of ibuprofen every eight hours and 40 mg. of Lasix three times per day via an automatic pump. He was also receiving 200 mg. of Tegretol twice per day.

Prior to his beginning the hospice care program, the patient's back pain had escalated and could not be resolved with morphine "bumps" prescribed for "break through" pain. Upon admission to the hospice unit, Michael required several "bumps" to achieve pain control. His wife stayed with him the first night because he did not want to be alone. He remained hospitalized for seven days. During that time Michael expressed to the hospice staff the need to "finish up some things" with his wife; he required extensive emotional support from both hospice staff and family.

After Michael's discharge, his care was managed well at home. He received 7.5 mg. of morphine per hour and began on methadone—10 mg. every 12 hours in addition to his morphine—because of increased discomfort. Three days after discharge, Michael also noted increased swelling and pain in the mid-back area with a nodule present that was expanding. With this expansion, Michael was having increased pain, and it was felt that he should see the physician who had placed the epidural catheter. At the clinic an abscess at the site of his laminectomy was discovered. An incision was made, and copious amounts of pus were drained. Michael was then readmitted to the hospice unit for intravenous antibiotic therapy, awaiting culture results. Leakage from the wound continued. He experienced continued escalation of significant pain in the back. Cultures demonstrated gram-positive bacteria in the wound; Michael had clearly developed an infection of the vertebrae. A decision was made to clean the wound. Upon surgical cleansing of his spine, the epidural catheter was removed, and the incision was left packed and open with dressing changes ordered twice daily. His surgical wound extended from the top of the shoulder blades to the waist along the spinal cord. The bony vertebrae and spinal column were exposed. Michael was placed on intravenous morphine with inadequate pain management. He called out in agonizing pain whenever the hospice staff irrigated his wound and did dressing changes. His morphine sulphate was increased by 30–50 mg. along with intravenous Valium 2–5 mg. with unsuccessful results. To enhance pain control the physician placed Michael on an air-fluidized bed that would achieve zero pressure.

As his condition slowly deteriorated, his family remained at his bedside, going home for periods of one or two hours daily. In the next eight days Michael's morphine was increased from 40 mg. per hour to 255 mg. per hour. However, he continued to be plagued by excruciating pain. During his agony the family became increasingly frustrated, exhausted, and overwhelmed.

They persistently begged the hospice staff to "do something" to help him be comfortable. The nurses expressed total frustration at their helplessness in the face of Michael's continued pleading of "Help me! Help me!" Even with massive doses of morphine and Valium he did not experience comfort.

—*Margaret Wolters, R.N.*

Case 3: Martha

Martha is a 49-year-old Hispanic American from a large South-western city with a sizable Hispanic population. A successful real estate agent, she is married to Joe and is the mother of one grown son, Larry, who lives in another state. Martha has always viewed herself as a spiritual person, interested in the varieties of the religious life; she attends a small Catholic church, the same one she and Joe have attended since they met at a party 30 years ago.

Martha has had a history of hypertension, and she recently quit smoking. She was brought into the emergency room of a private hospital near her home after suffering a stroke while reading the paper. The stroke, which left her marginally impaired, upset Joe tremendously. He had watched his mother care for his father, who had suffered a serious stroke, for almost two years before he died. The effects of the episode on Martha were slight, and she was discharged from the hospital after a week. A degree of facial paralysis caused her to slur her words, and she had some motor difficulty, but she was able to care for herself. She did take a leave of absence from her job.

Martha had always been hardworking and conscientious in her duties as a businessperson and parent. She and her husband had been looking forward to the time when they would be able to indulge their passion for traveling. Now, however, following the stroke, she became depressed and uncertain about her future. Concerned about another possible episode, she completed a living will, which in her state is nonbinding. She declared that she would want artificial supports withdrawn in case of an irreversible coma. Martha refused to place a DNR (do-not-resuscitate) order in her document. She was reluctant to discuss with her priest her fears about her own mortality, although she once told Joe that she was anxious about death, and that she wanted to die without pain.

A second, massive stroke left her in a coma. She was unresponsive to deep pain and showed no purposeful movement. Initially intubated as a precaution, she had been successfully weaned from the respirator. She was sustained, however, by a nasogastric feeding tube. Treatment continued for all complications: infections were treated with antibiotics, and gastrointestinal bleeding with blood transfusions. Her occasional respiratory distress was not serious enough for her to be placed back on the respirator. After two weeks, the consulting neurologist diagnosed Martha's condition as probably pervasive, permanent, and irreversible, commonly called a persistent vegetative state (PVS), pending a confirming examination one week later. The subsequent neurological exam confirmed the PVS diagnosis, and she was transferred from the coronary care unit to a floor, while the hospital social worker sought placement in a nursing home or an extended care facility.

In an ethics consultation held with their priest, their family lawyer, Martha's consulting and attending physicians, and the hospital's lawyer, Joe states that the present quality of his wife's life is so diminished that he wants the tube removed and all treatment stopped, despite the certainty of starvation. The hospital representatives suggest that a DNR order be entered in her medical records and the tube maintained. The lawyer points out that the state's Living Will Act forbids the removal of the tube if death would result "solely" from the withdrawal rather than from an existing terminal condition which could be interpreted to mean imminent death. Joe's lawyer, however, argues that the act defines as "terminal" a condition in which (1) death is imminent, and (2) death-delaying procedures serve only to prolong the dying process. Because the physicians believe that Martha's condition is permanent and that she could live for another 20 years with careful management, Joe is adamant that the use of the nasogastric tube be discontinued. The family priest is sincerely disturbed by the direction of the conversation and by Joe's request; he claims that each human life is a divine gift and that God teaches through the accidents and contingencies of life.

After lengthy debate, in light of Martha's advance directive, the legal precedent of a patient's right to refuse medical treatment, and the argument that death was imminent without the tube, the physicians agree to discontinue nutrition and hydration as medical treatment; the hospital lawyer concurs with the decision. The priest leaves, quite upset, declaring that "starvation is starvation." The tube is removed on the following day.

One day later, Joe, in the presence of two nurses, asks the physician to "do something" to hasten his wife's dying. He sees no point in "stretching things out." The physician replies that this lies beyond his professional responsibilities. Joe again asks him to do something, saying, "I'd do it myself, but I don't know how."

—Edwin R. DuBose

Case 4: Ron

Ron was diagnosed with Alzheimer's disease seven years ago. The 68-year-old father of six children, a husband for 47 years, he is a former president of a large accounting firm in the Midwest. Though he was born into an Orthodox Jewish family, following his marriage he and his wife dropped out of an active Jewish congregational life. Two of his children have been active in their faith tradition; the remainder see themselves as secularized Jews. At the death of his wife shortly before his retirement, the two children urged him to renew the practice of his faith, and although Ron occasionally attended services, his deteriorating condition intervened.

Because many disorders initially have similar symptoms, Alzheimer's was not suspected at first. When Ron began to miss appointments, his children attributed his forgetfulness to "old age setting in." They began to worry when he came home from work, changed clothes, and then changed back into a suit because "it was time to go to work." A neuropsychologist diagnosed early Alzheimer's; he told Ron that his general physical health was good, although he was developing the first symptoms of chronic arthritis. The physician explained that his mental condition would continue to deteriorate for perhaps as long as 15 years; the average survival period was 10 years. Deeply depressed, Ron retired shortly after his diagnosis. He angrily informed his children that he was capable of looking after himself and wanted to be independent as long as possible. Several months later, however, a son found him sitting in his car, upset because he could not remember how it operated. When Ron forgot to turn off a gas burner on his stove, the children persuaded him to give up his home of 20 years.

Three of the children agreed to rotate care for him in their homes. During his stay with his religious daughter, it was arranged for her rabbi to come by the house, but Ron could not remember the man from one visit to the next and was either unresponsive or agitated at his presence. When it became clear that their father required a consistent home environment, his son Robert took over primary responsibility for Ron's care and became his legal guardian. Because Robert was single, he depended heavily upon the other siblings for assistance.

Ron's sons and daughters had to look after him every day, 24 hours a day. All but Robert were married and had children; it was often difficult for Robert to arrange for continuous care and supervision. Occasionally the strain erupted into anger and recriminations; certainly Robert felt his responsibility very strongly and sometimes wondered how he could stand the stress of having his father in his home. However, the yearly cost of nursing home care averaged $30,000 in this state. The family discussed moving their father to another state where costs were slightly less, but the daughter living there was reluctant to take over guardianship from Robert. Finally, because of Ron's severe dementia and the burdens of home care, Robert and his siblings decided to admit their father to an extended care facility despite the cost. He was no longer able to recognize them, and the slightest change in routine upset him.

Nine months later Ron began to require spoon feeding. Now, after three more months in the facility, he has developed a persistent fever and diarrhea. For two weeks he has refused to eat and drink adequately and has lost 15 pounds. After discussion with Robert and one other son, and with their concurrence, the physician in the extended care facility decides against transferring Ron to an acute care hospital for diagnostic procedures. He writes a NO CPR order and instructs the staff to provide comfort care. Because Ron tends to wander, he must be restrained when unattended. Visiting his father, Robert increasingly finds himself remembering the active, vigorous man his father used to be. He curses God and asks what his father did to deserve this fate. He begins secretly to plan his father's death, perhaps through suffocation.

—Edwin R. DuBose

2

A BRIEF HISTORICAL PERSPECTIVE

Active voluntary euthanasia is not new to the latter part of the twentieth century. Even in ancient societies, terminally ill people requested to have their dying hastened, though the meaning of euthanasia for them differed from its meaning today. What seems new is the cultural context in which the question of euthanasia arises. Many factors contribute to this new context, but perhaps most influential are the sophistication and availability of medical technology and the social, scientific, moral, and religious beliefs that permeate modern American society. In many ways, the cases in Chapter 1 illustrate the new contexts in which the issue is raised.

This brief historical overview, limited to the Western tradition for purposes of this report, situates in a broader context the current debate in the United States about active voluntary euthanasia.

Throughout history the practice of ending human life has been intimately related to its moral acceptability, and in any specific period this has been influenced by a number of religious, moral, and social attitudes. As attitudes toward death have shifted, along with the value placed on individual life as compared to the good of the community, the meaning of euthanasia and the role of the physician in prolonging life or hastening death have also changed.[1] Therefore, to understand more fully the nuances of current ethical debate over active voluntary euthanasia, it is well to provide a historical survey of its conceptual origins.

Because the English word *euthanasia* is taken from the Greek *eu thanatos*, "good or easy death," this review begins with classical antiquity.[2]

Classical Antiquity

In the present day the term *euthanasia* is associated with the act of mercifully ending the life of a hopelessly suffering patient. The classical understanding of what is now called euthanasia, however, was broader in scope. Focusing on the act of hastening death, the contemporary question involving euthanasia tends to be, Is euthanasia under any conditions morally justifiable? For the ancients, in contrast, euthanasia did not necessarily imply an act, a means, or a method of causing or hastening death.[3] The focus was on one possible manner of dying, and the pivotal question was, Did the person voluntarily meet death with peace of mind and minimal pain? The Greeks sometimes employed the term to describe the "spiritual" state of the dying person at the impending moment of death; it was important that the person die a "good death," in a psychologically balanced state of mind, under composed circumstances, in a condition of self-control. To ensure such a death, it was permissible purposively to shorten a person's life.

Moreover, for the Greeks and Romans, a "good death" was not anchored in a medical context alone, nor did it carry the negative connotations we commonly attach to *suicide*.[4] Their stress was on the voluntary and reasoned nature of the dying, and they were generally sympathetic to active voluntary euthanasia, provided that the deed was done for the right reasons, for example, to end the suffering of a terminal illness.[5] In this sense, the English language has lost touch with many of the characteristic Greek and Roman understandings of active euthanasia, which tended to emphasize it as a mode of death, a way of dying, carefully distinguished from murder or what they judged to be morally unacceptable forms of suicide.

In classical antiquity, then, there was a generally recognized, although qualified, tolerance of the "freedom to leave," which permitted the sick or suffering to terminate their lives.[6] Furthermore, under the appropriate circumstances, it was permissible for others to administer the means of death.

On what grounds did some of the leading ancient philosophers support or oppose what is now called active voluntary euthanasia? Those who opposed it on religious grounds appealed directly to respect for human life, a moral principle derived from the logically prior religious principle that the gods valued each embodied soul. According to the Pythagoreans, earthly existence—including pain and possibly an agonizing death—was the gods' punishment for past sins. Therefore, bodily life must not be prematurely ended. Euthanasia was blameworthy because each embodied soul was ordered by the gods to serve out its natural life span; to desert one's station was tantamount to violating divine law. It is questionable whether human life was taken by the Pythagoreans to be valuable per se. Its value, though genuine and of binding importance, was a derivative value resting ultimately on religious considerations.[7]

Plato, on the other hand, sought to moderate the Pythagoreans' unconditional opposition to euthanasia. His view of suicide was generally negative, although he was sympathetic toward euthanasia in cases of agonizing and debilitating illness. In the *Phaedo*, for instance, he suggested that if death is imminent and irreversible, one may take early leave when no other course appears open.[8] More strongly, in the *Republic*, rejecting the argument that one owed his life to the gods and therefore had no right to end suffering, he linked and subordinated the value of the individual to the person's ability to perform his functions well for the state.[9] Plato therefore approved voluntary euthanasia for the incurably ill or disabled on utilitarian grounds, because the chronically ill were useless both to themselves and to the state.

One who disagreed with Plato's support of euthanasia was his former student Aristotle. In particular, Aristotle was opposed to the proposition that it was morally acceptable for a person suffering from an incurable illness or disability to take his life.[10] Unlike those who predicated their positions on religious grounds, he argued that citizens owed a duty to the state to remain productive citizens as long as possible. Thus a person was to face death bravely no matter what, contributing to the good of the state even in painful or debilitating circumstances. Euthanasia was blameworthy for Aristotle not simply because it deprived the state prematurely of one of its own but also because such an act typically constituted an excessive degree of rashness or cowardice. Dying courageously—by not willfully giving in to death even in the face of a terminal, debilitating disease—constituted a significant moral test for the virtuous person. Better that the person seek the mean of honorable conduct, even (perhaps especially) in the face of death, and thus become an example to others.

Roman attitudes toward euthanasia as a release from unendurable suffering reflected Greek influences. The Stoics, for instance, endorsed voluntary euthanasia as an option when a person's life, due to pain, illness, or physical abnormalities, was no longer in accordance with his or her individual felt needs and self-knowledge.[11] At least two conditions were necessary to justify euthanasia as a rational act: first, the person's motivation had to fit an appropriate category, for example, victimization by chronic or incurable disease; and second, the person had to weigh his or her responsibilities to others. Thus the Stoics wanted to ensure that euthanasia did not amount to an impulsive wish to escape life's legitimate duties.[12]

The question of physicians' moral responsibility to fulfill their patients' requests for easy deaths appeared early in the classical period. Socrates, according to Plato, saw painful disease and suffering as good reasons not to cling to life and opposed the physician's extending the natural dying process. He praised Asclepius, god of healing and medicine, for his more humane and practical policies: "He did not want to lengthen out good-for-nothing lives. . . . Those who are diseased . . . , [physicians] will leave to die, and the corrupt and incurable souls they will put an end to themselves."[13] How and whether physicians were able to determine "good-for-nothing" lives and "corrupt" souls requires a lengthier discussion. Apparently, however, many physicians dedicated to Asclepius practiced this policy, although alternative positions did exist.

For instance, the Hippocratic oath seems to forbid physicians' participation in acts designed to shorten life: "I will neither give a deadly drug to anybody if asked for it, nor will I make a suggestion to this effect."[14] It has been argued that the oath does not represent the ethical values of mainstream classical society but was a product of the esoteric ethical teachings of fourth-century B.C.E. Pythagoreanism with its religiously grounded prohibitions against prematurely ending life. Other scholars claim that this provision of the oath may have been intended as a tacit reminder to physicians that under no circumstances did their profession morally permit them to be an accomplice to murder. Given the general moral approval of a "good death," however, acting to end a patient's life, with that person's consent, was commonplace. It does appear that during antiquity many people preferred voluntary death to endless agony and that some physicians gave their patients the poisons for which they asked or administered them at the patient's request.[15]

In sum, religious, moral, and social prohibitions against active voluntary euthanasia did not reflect the dominant moral outlook or actual practices of the ancient Greek and Roman world. Euthanasia connoted a genuine concern for the psychological state of mind of the suffering person for whom life had become an intolerable burden. Moreover, in antiquity, moral evaluation of the person's decision (and of actions by the one supplying his or her medical services) was linked to the precondition that the patient was free to make a reasoned decision regarding the option to hasten his or her death and was not acting out of cowardice or a desire to avoid life's legitimate duties.

Because of this moral acceptance of active voluntary euthanasia under certain circumstances, Greek and Roman physicians typically did not feel that they had to prolong human life. It was the physician's role to support the patient in the dying process, to help ensure for him or her a good death. Given the views on euthanasia's virtues in the face of chronic to terminal disease, what is now termed active euthanasia was not widely prohibited. According to medical historian Paul Carrick," [Not] until Christian values became dominant in the last century and a half of the Roman Empire, did the moral prohibition against euthanasia gain support in ancient medical circles and society."[16]

The Christian Era

For the Romans and the Greeks, dying decently and rationally mattered immensely. In a sense, how they died was a measure of the final value of life, especially for a life wasted by disease and suffering. For early Christians, however, only God had the right to give and take life, active euthanasia was viewed as an illicit exercise of a divine prerogative.[17]

Generally, the practice of active euthanasia among the sick became unusual after about the second century C.E., because of the growing acceptance of the importance placed by Judeo-Christian teachings upon individual life and the endurance of suffering. By the fifth century, Augustine held that life and its suffering were divinely ordained by God and must be borne accordingly.[18] A human was created in the image of God, and his or life thus belonged to God; the time and manner of death was God's will and God's only. Moreover, as the writings of the New Testament assumed canonical form, suffering was viewed by Christians as something in which they could rejoice for two reasons: (1) God used suffering as a means of producing spiritual maturity; and (2) the very fact that Christians endured suffering was proof that they were children of God.[19] Christians were to engage in an active, direct ministry of consolation and encouragement of their fellow sufferers. The relief to be provided was not removal of the suffering but a consolation that transformed the suffering into a positive force in the person's life. Thus the belief developed that one should not abandon the life assigned to him or her by God but should endure it in the hope of a certain resurrection. These influences helped to shape social, moral, and religious attitudes toward illness and disability and acceptance of suffering at the time of death. As the ethic of respect for human life achieved this moral status, the early Christians declared it the absolute standard of right conduct for doctor and patient alike. Finally, although Christian charity brought a heightened sense of responsibility to relieve suffering, the biblical commandment against killing seemed to prohibit absolutely the taking of a person's life even to relieve suffering.[20]

During the next eight centuries, views of euthanasia were shaped by moral and legal prohibitions endorsed by the authority of the Catholic church.[21] In the thirteenth century, Thomas Aquinas argued that shortening one's life was sinful not only because it violated a commandment but because it left no time for the person's repentance. Also, taking one's own life or the life of another was against the law of nature and contrary to charity. Such an act was not lawful because every person belonged to the community, and it was a sin against God because life was a gift and subject only to God's powers.[22] Given the Christian proscriptions against active euthanasia for any reason, the sense of a "good death" was reinterpreted: the Christian was supposed to be tranquil and accepting at death. The means by which this acceptance was to be achieved included primarily physical comfort, moral support, and prayer. This essentially passive process was largely independent of the physician; the clergy, family, and friends prepared the patient for a good, "Christian" death.

A theoretical discussion of active euthanasia was presented by Sir Thomas More in his *Utopia*, first published in 1516. In his vision of the ideal society, "if a disease is not only incurable but also distressing and agonizing without cessation, then the priests and the public officials exhort the man . . . to free himself from this bitter life . . . or else voluntarily permit others to free him."[23] Although the English term had not yet been coined, More clearly described the active form of euthanasia. In his essay he offered no discussion of the physician's role; he did outline, however, certain precautions to be taken to avoid possible abuses of the practice.

More's comments on euthanasia are significant when viewed against the religious, social, and political climate of this general period. As gathering theological storm clouds gave way to Luther's thundering against Rome, one's understanding of Christian faith became crucially important. The reformers in the reign of Henry VIII, to whom More succumbed, and later those in Elizabeth's reign, faced a formidable task in converting the people to Protestantism. Following an Augustinian argument against euthanasia as an evil caused by a lack of faith, they viewed euthanasia as the antithesis of the faith that every Christian needed in order to be saved; it represented the opposite of pious hope. Their hostility to euthanasia also was aroused by the contemporary revival of Greek and Roman ideas that excused and even glorified voluntary euthanasia in certain circumstances; the reformers looked instead to the New Testament for guidance. As Renaissance humanism came under scrutiny, the medical cosmology inherited from the Middle Ages validated the reformers' antipathy to euthanasia: human beings' susceptibility to disease was the consequence of the Fall, and any illness might be punishment for an individual's sin.[24] The call to endure the suffering of illness or disability in repentance and "in good faith" acted as a counterbalance to the practice of active euthanasia. An "easy death" became a temptation to be resisted.

At the same time, however, Renaissance humanism retained its influence in the area of medical science. The recovery of interest in classical antiquity had spurred Christian medicine to concentrate anew on the natural order and had effected a change in the medieval understanding of euthanasia: A "good death" became a "natural" death. Here "natural" connoted a better or higher kind of death, the result of a temperate life or a cultivated acceptance of death as God's will. In this context, physical pain and suffering was caused by unnatural activity or by disease. The role of the Christian physician was to help the patient recover a natural, spiritual life, thereby prolonging life and enabling an easy death in the fullness of time. Displaying this Christian humanist orientation toward humankind's dignity and well-being, in the seventeenth century Francis Bacon advocated the use of science and medicine to control bodily processes, either to lengthen life or, when indicated, to end it painlessly. Euthanasia increasingly came to be identified with specific measures taken by the physician to relieve suffering, including for some the possibility of hastening death.[25] However, despite the promise of planned experimental research to control bodily processes and relieve suffering, the physician was not the dominant figure in the death chamber until the nineteenth century, when scientific advances began to erode the theological monopoly that had developed over the centuries.[26]

The Nineteenth Century

The role of the physician in dealing with the dying patient received significant attention in the early nineteenth century. During the previous decades, the enthusiasms of the Enlightenment faith in human progress led to the elaboration of a number of ambitious, this-worldly alternatives to Christian attitudes toward illness, suffering, and death. Because of the human ability to know and control the natural, physical world, a number of Enlightenment philosophers believed that biomedical research, public health programs, and progressive thinking would result in a much extended life span. Now that science had been freed from religion's superstition and ignorance, Benjamin Franklin predicted, the new scientific and medical advances would make possible human longevity of a thousand years or more.[27] In spite of this optimism, however, by 1800 the limits of medical achievement were recognized. Medicine, it was argued, could not conquer death, but the physician could marshal medicine's forces to slow down the tragically inevitable process of decline. As part of the effort to ward off premature death, new devices were developed to prevent pain and relieve distress, and these required the expert intervention and guidance of the medical profession and inaugurated the age of heroic medicine.[28]

This new level of medical intervention to prolong life prompted the criticism that physicians were needlessly prolonging the dying process. A number of articles written in Europe and America during the late eighteenth and early nineteenth centuries criticized physicians who treated diseases rather than patients. Many of these pieces discussed the role of the physician in promoting the classical notion of harmonious death. After noting the tendency of physicians to neglect a patient once an illness was found to be terminal, the author of one article in 1826 urged doctors to accept responsibility for their patients' "spiritual" euthanasia. Physical and moral comfort were to be provided, but heroic medications likely to prolong the dying and extend a person's suffering were to be avoided. At the same time, the author condemned the thought of hastening a patient's death.[29] However, medical and therapeutic advances during the century made heroic intervention increasingly possible and set the stage for open advocacy of the practice of active euthanasia.

Among these developments were advances in the diagnosis of disease which, combined with a more rational understanding of disease processes, permitted more accurate prognoses for patients. The introduction of statistical methods into medicine and the emphasis on pathological correlations with clinical conditions allowed physicians to predict with some confidence a patient's course. Theoretical and practical advances in pain relief were also made. Although drugs with efficacy in relieving pain had been known and used for centuries, the isolation of morphine and the development of the hypodermic syringe in the mid-1800s allowed potent analgesics to be administered in accurate doses and by a route through which their action was very rapid. These developments encouraged an emphasis on the palliation of disease and the comfort of the patient at the time of death. Such agents used to ease suffering were soon openly advocated by others for the practice of active euthanasia for reasons of mercy.[30]

Samuel D. Williams, schoolmaster and essayist, in 1870 published the first paper to deal entirely with the concept of active voluntary euthanasia and its application.[31] There he advocated active euthanasia for all willing patients with incurable and painful diseases. Williams further argued that it was the duty of medical attendants, presumably physicians, to provide active euthanasia to their patients. Neither concern that pain and suffering should be nobly borne until a natural death nor the sense that one's life belonged to God entered his argument.

By the beginning of the twentieth century, the major elements in the contemporary arguments for and against the practice of active voluntary euthanasia had been articulated. The growth of scientific knowledge and technology led to a reconsideration of traditional moral views, accompanied by a decline in the importance of theology in shaping social views of suicide and euthanasia. Some physicians admitted having practiced active euthanasia, and others expressed sympathy for the practice. Other physicians, however, found no medical precedent to justify the sacrifice of life and believed that the practice would lead to abuses, and, being illegal, would be regarded as murder.[32] Many others continued to see life as God's gift, not to be taken lightly or curtailed prematurely. Thus many people believed that the issue could not be settled in light of moral and religious concerns, and more attention was given to its legal aspects. As a compromise, some people began to advocate what they called *passive* euthanasia. At that time, the term referred to the avoidance of extreme or heroic measures to prolong life in cases of incurable and painful illness; advocates maintained the treatment should be withheld not to hasten death but to avoid the pain and suffering of prolonged dying. This development paved the way for more contemporary controversies surrounding the issue of *withdrawing* medical treatment, which today is associated with the term *passive euthanasia*.[33]

The line between active killing for mercy and withdrawing or withholding medical treatment has been, until recently, a critical part of an ethic for the care of the terminally or critically ill. With recent cases in which decisions to withdraw medically supplied nutrition and hydration are legally sanctioned, people are raising questions about the viability of sharp moral and legal distinction between passive and active voluntary euthanasia.[34]

—*Edwin R. DuBose*

3

SOME QUESTIONS AND ANSWERS

People ask a variety of questions relating to euthanasia and the many issues associated with it. These questions concern the underlying causes of current interest and debate, the meaning of frequently used terms, and societal attitudes and responses. We attempt to address some of these questions and concerns in the pages that follow. Our purpose is to give an overview of the issue while at the same time providing some conceptual resources for thinking about it. As you read, we suggest that you keep in mind the cases from Chapter 1.

Because this presentation is meant to be introductory, we have sought to avoid the intricacies and subtleties of the many controversies surrounding distinctions that can be made. Not all will agree with the explanation of the language of euthanasia given in these pages. Certainly there are other ways of defining terms and describing the realities involved. Readers would do well to refer to the bibliography for references that might reflect alternative viewpoints.

1. There's much talk about active euthanasia these days. It's in the media, grass-roots movements in several states are seeking to have legislation enacted to legalize it, we find discussions of it in medical journals, ethicists are talking about it in their meetings and publications, it's becoming more and more a topic of ordinary conversation. Why now?

There are any number of reasons. Cases appearing in newspaper headlines have put euthanasia on our minds, and it's likely that others will in the future. Two events in the summer of 1990 generated lots of conversation—the Janet Adkins case and the U.S. Supreme Court decision in the case of Nancy Cruzan. In the former, Janet Adkins solicited the help of Dr. Jack Kevorkian and his "suicide machine" to bring about a "gentle and easy death" rather than face the horrors of Alzheimer's disease. In the latter, the Supreme Court ruled that states can require the highest level of evidence to ascertain the supposed wishes of persons who have permanently lost their capacity to make decisions about medical treatment. Because Nancy Cruzan had not left clear and convincing evidence of her wishes, the Missouri Supreme Court would not allow the termination of the artificial feeding keeping her alive, even though she was totally unaware and in a persistent vegetative state. The first situation illustrates what can happen when people fear the ravages of disease and the medical technology that can keep them alive to suffer through it. The second feeds the fear of many that they will lose control over their dying. Euthanasia is seen by some as a way of dealing with these realities. In towns everywhere, less publicized cases generate the same fears and much discussion.

2. Are there any other reasons that people are concerned about this issue now?

Probably most people in our society have had some experience of medical technology's great successes. As never before, technology is able to save and prolong life and cure disease, sometimes in very dramatic ways. But there's a reverse side. It is often used inappropriately and at a high price. People can become victims of technology and have their dying prolonged beyond what is reasonable or their lives extended at an extremely low quality. Medical technology can burden people with machines, procedures, tubes, and medications rather than enhance their well-being.

What we may be seeing today is a loss of faith in the medical utopias promised a generation ago. The early transplant surgeons were cultural heroes. We were told that exotic discoveries and instruments would enhance life in every way. Now we are taking a second look. Still turning to medical advances with hope, we find they have not removed what someone has called "the terror of limitlessness." By prolonging life "artificially," they may often have increased the terror. The interest in euthanasia shows that people are trying to deal with these conflicts.

3. It seems as though fear is a major driving force. Is it?

Yes. People fear that they will not be taken seriously as persons, that their rights will be slighted, that others will do things that violate their sense of the meaning of life, that someone else will control them. Coupled with this, of course, is the fear of death itself.

4. Is it fear only of medicine's successes in maintaining life that's at issue here?

No. Medicine's *limits* also fuel the interest in euthanasia. Medicine cannot cure all diseases, or even suppress or alleviate the symptoms of some diseases. People fear mental deterioration, the wasting away of their bodies, the embarrassment of disfigurement, the sapping of energy, the loss of control and the ability to do things for themselves, the physical pain, and the many forms of psychological anguish. Many of these fears are evidenced in at least three of the cases that opened this discussion. Euthanasia can do what medicine can't.

Also, people are living longer. And with longer life come additional years of physical and, for many, mental decline. Years of chronic illness add to the burden for some. Always looming on the horizon is the specter of finishing one's days in a nursing home. Medicine to date has not been able to halt the aging process and all that it brings. Again, euthanasia might be seen as a way of achieving what medicine can't.

5. Are there any other driving forces?

Another contributing factor is the great emphasis in our society on the "right to choose for oneself" or "freedom of choice"—in technical terms, *autonomy*. This translates to "It's my life to do with as I please, to live out in accordance with my own beliefs, values, personality, and style." Euthanasia is regarded by some as the "ultimate choice." It gives one a say in when and how one is going to die. It provides the individual with control over dying. One's dying can be "self-managed" instead of being left to the decisions of others, and to nature or God, as in the case of Steve in Chapter 1. So underlying the talk about rights and choice is a very keen concern about control. Who is going to control the decision about when and how I die? Who controls my destiny near the point of death? Much of the fear has to do with precisely this: do I lose control?

This concern raises complex philosophical and theological questions. Do we really have complete control over our lives? Do our lives belong to us to do with as we wish? Are there limits to our freedom to choose for ourselves? Does autonomy extend to actively ending one's life? Does so much emphasis on the right of the individual to decide give short shrift to our interconnectedness? Does it overlook responsibilities to family members, to the communities in which we live, and to society as a whole? These are at bottom questions about *meaning*—the meaning of rights, of autonomy, of relatedness to others and to the Other.

6. Are there other issues of similar import?

There are. In fact, there are several. What, for example, does *life* mean for a human being? Can human life be equated with mere biological functioning? Or is something else essential to *human* life? This raises the question of *personhood*. What does it mean to be a person? Can one cease being a person while still in some sense being *alive*? And what do we mean by *quality of life*? At what point, if any, is human life no longer worth continuing for the individual whose life it is? This question arises in some sense in each of our four cases.

How are we to understand human finitude, that is, the fact that our lives and abilities are limited? What meaning do we give to dependency on others, to decline and aging, to pain and suffering, to illness and death, to human existence as a whole? Some observers claim that we are experiencing a crisis about the meaning of life, and partly for that reason, euthanasia is seen as an effective remedy for dealing with some of life's negativities.

7. What about religion? Does religion figure into an increased interest in euthanasia?

It probably does. Some would say that a weakening in some fundamental religious beliefs, particularly those having to do with the existence of God, or the relationship of God to human beings and of human beings to God, or an afterlife, can contribute to support for euthanasia. If there is no God, then one's life is not seen as a gift of the Creator but entirely as one's own. If people are not responsible to an ultimate Other, then the scope of individual autonomy increases. Religiously based injunctions against taking innocent human life lose their force. And if there is no afterlife, one need not worry about ultimate accountability for engaging in euthanasia.

8. What about religious believers? Do they sometimes support euthanasia?

Yes. We're seeing changes here, changes in certain religious and moral beliefs rather than a rejection of them. Some people, for example, acknowledge that human life is a gift of the Creator and that humans are caretakers of that life—it is not theirs to do with as they wish. Yet ending human life, under certain circumstances, is not outside the scope of responsible stewardship. Euthanasia is viewed by some as a form of stewardship of life and as a legitimate exercise of human intelligence and choice.

31

Some maintain that euthanasia should not be lumped with other forms of prohibited killing. The motive for the killing is different; the circumstances surrounding it are different. The moral evil present in other forms of taking innocent life may not be present here. Hastening someone's dying at their request does not seem to be morally the same as depriving someone of future life against their will for such reasons as greed, revenge, jealousy, and hatred.

So there is a degree of receptivity to euthanasia even among some who would consider themselves religious believers. We've noted just some of the changes. The challenge to religious communities in the months and years ahead will be to confront these and other new directions head-on and honestly, and to assess them critically.

9. Have religious communities staked out positions on the issue?

Religious groups do have long traditions of belief and practice regarding death and dying and the taking of human life. They also have long-standing beliefs about the sacredness of life, the nature of human beings, suffering, salvation, the existence of an afterlife, the existence of a deity, and the deity's relation to humankind. These and other basic beliefs inform their thinking about euthanasia. In addition to their traditions of belief and their centuries-long interest in the issues, religious communities also bring to the discussion a moral wisdom forged over the centuries. For these reasons we are including in this report an overview of the attitudes of various contemporary religious groups. The religious voice is and will be an important voice in the debate that lies ahead.

A word of caution, however. Not all members of a particular group hold a uniform position on euthanasia. Some people very much believe in the sacredness of life yet are rethinking their position on euthanasia. Also, it could be that in the years ahead some groups modify their stance.

10. But how widespread could this interest in active euthanasia actually be? Is what we're seeing actually a media effect or are more people really thinking this way?

That's difficult to answer. The polls seem to indicate that a considerable proportion of the population approves of euthanasia. In a New York Times/CBS News poll of 573 adults conducted by telephone June 6 and 7, 1990 (with a sampling-error margin of plus or minus four percentage points), 53 percent of the individuals contacted believed that a doctor should be allowed to assist an ill person in taking his or her own life. 42 percent said no, and 6 percent weren't sure or gave no answer. Among the 53 percent, younger adults, males, and liberals made up the largest groups.

These findings are supported by an independent poll of 1,213 adults nationwide conducted for the Times Mirror Center for the People and the Press and released on June 10, 1990. According to the survey, seven in ten adults believe it is justified in some circumstances for a person to kill his or her spouse, if the spouse is suffering from terrible pain from a terminal illness. One in five believes it is never justified. 49 percent of those surveyed (compared with 40 percent in 1975) think that someone with an incurable disease has a moral right to suicide and 55 percent (compared to 41 percent in 1975) believe that someone suffering great pain with no hope of improvement has a moral right to suicide. 57 percent oppose suicide because the patient is a burden on the family, while 59 percent oppose it because life has become a burden to the patient. Acceptance of suicide is more widespread among younger people (58 percent of those 30-49) than older (39 percent of those 65 and older). The survey found that most born-again Christians and very religious people reject a right to suicide for reasons of terminal illness, but are rather evenly divided regarding suicide when the patient is in great pain. Paradoxically, a majority of born-again Christians and very religious people believe that "mercy killing" by spouses is sometimes justified, though it is not endorsed.

In 1989 the Chicago-based National Opinion Research

Council found that 68.7 percent of Americans sampled agreed with the statement that doctors should be allowed by law to end a patient's life by some painless means, if the person has an incurable disease and if the patient and family request it. This represented an increase from 62.4 percent in 1977.

In a 1987 California poll by Mervin Field, 64 percent responded yes to the question, "Should an incurably ill patient have the right to ask for and get life-ending medication?" 27 percent answered no, and 9 percent were undecided.

Similar results emerged in a 1990 Roper poll commissioned by the Hemlock Society. Asked "When a person has a painful and distressing terminal disease, do you think doctors should or should not be allowed by law to end the patient's life if there is no hope of recovery and the patient requests it?" 64 percent replied yes, 24 percent no, and 13 percent either weren't sure or gave no answer.

The 1977 National Opinion Research Council poll also showed that of those who described themselves as having a weak religiosity 23.5 percent opposed active euthanasia, while 76.5 percent approved. Among those who described themselves as strongly religious, however, 50.5 percent said no and 49.5 percent responded yes. This suggests that religious beliefs do play some role in people's attitudes toward euthanasia.

By contrast, the 1990 Roper poll indicates little difference between those who identify with a religious tradition (64.6 percent yes) and those who don't (65 percent yes), as well as very little difference among major religious denominations (Protestant 65 percent, Catholic 62 percent, Jewish 70 percent responding yes).

Polls of course are tricky. Their accuracy depends on what questions are asked, how they are asked, the circumstances in which they are asked, who is asked, and how the questions are understood. Nevertheless, these results may be somewhat indicative of what people are thinking.

11. People who oppose or who are unsure about euthanasia often talk about the "slippery slope." What's that all about?

"Slippery slope" is simply a way of saying that once a person or society starts down a certain path, gravity will pull them further along it. Applied to euthanasia, it means that if we allow physicians (or other agents) to end the lives of the imminently dying at their request, it won't stop there. We will be drawn further down the path to include other categories of individuals—terminal but nondying patients, incurable but nonterminal patients (or who are in a persistent vegetative state), handicapped newborns, the senile, the mentally handicapped, and so on.

12. Could you be a bit more specific about this?

Well, suppose active euthanasia is legalized as a valid expression of personal autonomy and in order to relieve the pain and suffering of dying patients. Wouldn't it also be logical to legalize euthanasia for those who are terminally ill but not yet dying (for example, individuals with Huntington's disease, multiple sclerosis, or Lou Gehrig's disease or even in the early stages of cancer or AIDS) or for those who are incurable but nonterminal (for example, individuals who are left severely impaired after an accident, dialysis patients, those with diabetes, or who are quadriplegic, or who have suffered a severe stroke, or who are in a persistent vegetative state). They have longer to live and so a longer time to suffer. If it makes sense to relieve a short period of suffering for the dying patient, wouldn't it make even more sense to relieve a longer span of suffering for the nondying but terminal or incurable? Furthermore, why should the exercise of autonomy be limited to requests during the dying phase of an illness.

13. So we've expanded euthanasia to the nonterminal and the incurable. Is this where the line gets drawn?

Well, why stop here? Why not also include those who are suffering from loss of their mental capacities? Why shouldn't people suffering from Alzheimer's, for example, be able to exercise their autonomy in the form of an advance directive (a living will) or a durable power of attorney and request to have their life ended when they become incompetent and their quality of life is severely compromised?

Then what about those who are no longer able to make decisions for themselves but have not made provisions in advance? Shouldn't they also have the opportunity to have their pain and suffering relieved? The doctrine of "substituted judgment" could be applied here. It could be said that so-and-so would not want to live this poor quality of life and would choose assistance in ending his or her life were he or she now able. There is a shift here from voluntary to nonvoluntary euthanasia. But why not? Why should those who are incompetent be deprived of relief?

And if substituted judgment can serve as a legitimizing basis for euthanasia, why not also "best interests" (though here it must be said, the argument from patient autonomy is not as strong)? If there are no substantial indications of what a person would have chosen were he or she able, might not decision-makers argue that it is in that individual's "best interests" to have his or her life ended? And if this is applicable to adults, why not also to handicapped newborns and to terminally ill children? Or why not the mentally ill to relieve their mental anguish?

So you see, what some fear is that one step onto the slope of voluntary active euthanasia might lead, logically and in practice, to a slide down the slope to include more and more categories of individuals, even to the point of legitimizing nonvoluntary euthanasia. Of course, the most serious scenario would be to allow for the practice of involuntary euthanasia, that is, ending a person's life against their will.

14. Isn't euthanasia legal in Holland? If it's not a big problem there, why should it be here?

There's a fair amount of misunderstanding regarding euthanasia in Holland. First, it is not legal even though it is practiced. There are no reliable data on how widespread the practice is. Some estimate between 2,000 and 10,000 cases per year out of a population of 15 million.

Second, it is practiced only in exceptional circumstances and following strict criteria: (1) the request for euthanasia must be entirely voluntary, free of all external coercion, and must originate from the patient (this presupposes that the patient's request is well-considered and persistent); (2) the patient's suffering, of whatever type, must be intolerable and without prospect of improvement (so, in a sense, euthanasia is a last resort, other alternatives having been considered and found wanting); (3) it must be performed by a physician who has first consulted with a physician colleague who has experience in this area.

Under the current Dutch penal code, euthanasia is illegal, and a physician practicing it could be punished by up to 12 years in prison. Either the coroner or physician must report to the police that euthanasia has occurred. The police in turn report to the district attorney, who then decides whether or not to prosecute. In all the cases that were prosecuted between 1973 and 1983, the first two conditions above were deemed essential by judges who reached verdicts of not guilty, acquittal, or conditional punishments. They were also the conditions that permitted district attorneys to dismiss such cases. The third criterion was mentioned as important by some courts and judges. Since 1984, all three criteria have been employed by all courts, and they have gradually developed into the necessary conditions for the acceptable or tolerable (though not legal) practice of active euthanasia.

In 1984, the Royal Dutch Medical Association endorsed these three conditions as essential requirements for any performance of euthanasia by a physician. Then, in 1985, the Netherlands State Commission on Euthanasia, formed to make concrete recommendations to the government for law and jurisprudence in this area, issued its report. One of its recommendations was that euthanasia should not be punishable by law when carried out according to the above conditions. A debate that should have occurred in Parliament in 1989 never materialized because the coalition government fell. Until the matter is resolved legally, physicians, hospitals, and other health care institutions are attempting to protect themselves by developing and following policies that will make district attorneys less inclined to prosecute.

So it would be far more accurate to say that a certain professional and public tolerance exists in Holland with regard to euthanasia, though it certainly is not accepted by all and is not legal. Also, there is a general social awareness that much remains to be debated ethically and legally. Because of the lack of "hard data" there is really no way of telling whether there have been abuses or whether in practice there is any move down the "slippery slope." And, finally, because the Netherlands is so different from the United States—in its health care system and in its social, political, and legal milieu—its approach to euthanasia cannot be transposed to this country. It is important to note, for example, that neither pain management nor hospice care is as developed as it might be in Holland. This could account in part for the strong interest in euthanasia.

15. But don't people have a right to die?

The phrase "right to die" is actually quite ambiguous. It could mean several things. It could refer to the "right to refuse treatment" or the "right to be allowed to die," that is, the right not to have one's dying interfered with, the right to be free from the imposition of unwanted medical procedures. There is generally little disagreement about this right. It is recognized morally and legally.

But the "right to die" could also mean the "right to kill oneself," to commit suicide without the interference of others.

To date, such a right has no legal recognition. Many would still argue that it is a moral right flowing from our right to self-determination and autonomy. This implies certain views not only about autonomy but also about one's body and life and one's relationships to others. There is considerable disagreement about the existence of such a right.

Finally, the expression "right to die" is sometimes used to suggest a right to be killed by another at one's own request. This would be a claim for a right to voluntary active euthanasia. And this is precisely one of the major areas of disagreement in the euthanasia debate. Not only does it raise the issues associated with the previous interpretation; it also raises the question whether one can insist, as a matter of right, that another kill oneself or whether consensual homicide should be made legal.

16. The terms used in these discussions are all very confusing. I hear talk about euthanasia, terminating treatment, active euthanasia, passive euthanasia, assisted suicide. *Do these all mean the same thing, or are there really some differences?*

Important question. Often people use the term *euthanasia* when what they're referring to is really something quite different. Let's try to shed a bit of light on our language.

Suppose that Steve, the person with AIDS in the first case, had been placed on a respirator and also had a feeding tube inserted into his stomach to provide him with nourishment. His condition is such that without these measures he would die. Even with them, his condition continues to deteriorate, but more slowly. Steve eventually insists that the respirator and the feeding tube—both forms of "life-prolonging"/"life-sustaining" treatment—be removed, and that when he experiences cardiac or respiratory arrest, he not be resuscitated. Would stopping these measures and not resuscitating be considered euthanasia? In this case, they're *not*.

Why? Because terminating treatment here is a recognition that the treatment is doing the patient little or no good. It will not restore him to good health, and it is only prolonging the dying process. Furthermore, the burdens of the treatment (physical, psychological, social, economic) and possibly the diminished quality of his life (pain and suffering, severe physical or mental impairments) may outweigh the benefits, if any, to be derived from those treatments or the benefits for him of continued existence. While most religious traditions recognize a responsibility for preserving life, they also recognize that there are limits to that responsibility. A person need not do what is futile or unreasonable.

This insight is usually referred to as the principle of "burden/benefit" or "proportionate/disproportionate means." It is generally agreed that for a medical treatment to be morally obligatory there must be some proportion between burdens and benefits hoped for or obtained. Until fairly recently, this principle was called the principle of "ordinary/extraordinary means."

So the decision to stop treatment is really a decision to stop doing what is no longer of real benefit to the patient and what has become unreasonably burdensome, in order to allow nature to run its course. The intention is to stop interfering with the dying process, to step aside and allow the dying to happen. These kinds of decisions—whether about initiating or discontinuing treatment—are referred to as *termination of treatment, withholding/withdrawing life-sustaining treatment, refusal of life-extending treatment,* and *allowing to or letting die.* Some use the term "passive euthanasia" here, but it only adds to confusion and probably should be avoided.

17. Why shouldn't the term passive euthanasia be used? Refusing life-sustaining treatment sounds like a form of euthanasia.

The difference between passive euthanasia and forgoing life-sustaining treatment or allowing to die is a very complex matter about which there is considerable disagreement. It probably wouldn't be useful to venture into all the intricacies of the issue here. Nevertheless, some general comments can be made, provided we keep in mind that not all would agree.

Voluntary euthanasia is actually a form of suicide; it is taking one's own life, albeit with the assistance *(assisted suicide)* or the intervention *(euthanasia)* of another. Suicide requires that an individual (1) *intend their own death* and (2) *act in such a way as to bring it about.* If an individual intended to die, and refused treatment that was both beneficial and not seriously burdensome, that *would* constitute passive suicide or passive euthanasia. The refusal of treatment would simply be the means of causing death. And it would violate the moral obligation we have to do what is beneficial and reasonable in preserving our lives.

Take, for example, a person who has serious problems with chemical abuse and as a consequence has lost his job and destroyed his family and is now severely depressed. He suffers a heart attack that is likely to be fatal unless properly treated. He refuses all care. This may well be passive euthanasia, if the individual is intending his death by refusing treatment that would be beneficial and would not be excessively burdensome.

This is different from the individual who forgoes medical treatment because it provides no reasonable hope of benefit to his or her total well-being or will impose grave burdens or both. The primary intention in these cases is not to cause death but rather to avoid having to go through what is ultimately futile or what may seriously compromise physical, psychological, spiritual, or economic well-being, realizing that a consequence of treatment refusal will probably be an earlier death. While an earlier death is foreseen, it is not directly intended. This individual's decision is really a decision to acquiesce to the dying process because it is no longer reasonable to delay the inevitable.

18. So then, *what's* passive euthanasia?

Well, before talking about passive euthanasia, we should probably first talk about euthanasia in general and active euthanasia in particular. The word *euthanasia* is a combination of two Greek words that when put together mean "a good death." It has come to mean the direct taking of the life of a terminally ill or dying person for reasons of compassion. When intentionally ending life to relieve suffering is achieved by *doing something* (injecting the patient with potassium chloride, for example), we refer to it as *active euthanasia*. Whereas if it is achieved by *not doing* something that would have been beneficial to the patient in preserving life and not seriously burdensome, we call it *passive euthanasia* (for example, an accident victim who refuses respiratory support that is absolutely needed to sustain life but is needed only for such time as he or she is restored to full health). Passive euthanasia is actually an instance of passive suicide.

And, by the way, the use of pain medications in such a quantity that it leads to an earlier death should generally not be considered euthanasia. Think back to the second case. Michael is in excruciating pain despite a morphine dosage of 255 mg. per hour. Suppose the dosage were increased to the point where his pain was relieved, but a side effect was the suppression of his respirations, and his eventual death. If the intention here is to relieve pain and not to cause death, it would not be considered active euthanasia. Michael's death was foreseen as a possible consequence of increased dosage, but it was not directly intended.

19. I hear about other types of euthanasia besides "active" and "passive." What are they?

Well, euthanasia can take various forms. It can be accomplished with the consent of (and usually at the request of) the patient, in which case it is *active voluntary euthanasia*. In essence, voluntary euthanasia is suicide even though it is achieved either with the help of another or by another. When it is carried out by the individual him or herself, but with the assistance of someone else, particularly with regard to the means of achieving death, it's called *assisted suicide*. The Janet Adkins–Dr. Kevorkian case is an instance of this form of euthanasia. Janet Adkins pushed the button that led to her death, but Dr. Kevorkian provided the "suicide machine." But suppose a patient is too weak or otherwise unable to bring about his or her death and requests someone else (a physician, family member, or friend) to do so. This is *euthanasia in its strictest sense*, or *active voluntary euthanasia*.

Euthanasia can also be achieved against the will of the patient. This is *involuntary euthanasia*. Or it can be achieved without the consent of the patient. This would be *nonvoluntary euthanasia*. A family member of a person with Alzheimer's, for example, might end the life of the individual out of compassion, but without having obtained the person's consent. This would be somewhat illustrated by the fourth case where Robert contemplates ending his father's life. Though Ron is conscious, he probably does not have the capacity to understand or to make decisions on his own behalf. Terminating his life would be done without his consent. Or the family of someone in a persistent vegetative state could decide to take active measures to end the individual's life, with the patient having no say in the matter. Martha's case would be an example of this. Joe, her husband, wanted her physician to "do something" to hasten her dying even though the feeding tube had been removed to allow her to die. Martha had indicated in her advance directive that she didn't want life-sustaining treatment employed were she ever in a persistent vegetative state, but she had said nothing about having her life terminated.

What's really at issue in the growing debate is the legalization of active voluntary euthanasia. There may also be efforts to legalize assisted suicide. Assisting someone with suicide is illegal, though suicide itself is usually not. These are the areas where the moral and religious debates will also have to occur.

20. You mention legislation. Are there pressures to legislate?

Yes, and they are likely to increase. We see efforts at legislation in states like Washington, Oregon, Florida, and California spurred by grass-roots movements.

The current Supreme Court is tossing more and more decisions into the laps of state legislatures. Representatives and senators who didn't ask to address these kinds of moral questions are under great pressure, often from interest groups, to do so. Many have already been drawn in by the abortion issue and by the issues of advance directives (living wills and durable power of attorney for health care) and legislation on determination of death.

Then there's the public response—pro and con—to the case of Janet Adkins and the Kevorkian "suicide machine." The event itself and all the media attention have propelled the issue into people's awareness and even generated some sense of urgency. For many, on both sides of the issue, all this translates into a push to legislate! legislate!

21. What's so bad about legislation?

At some point, we'll probably need some kind of legislation. But it may be premature to move in that direction now. There is a real danger in forging ahead with legislation without having considered assisted suicide and especially active voluntary euthanasia in all their breadth and depth. Too much is at stake whichever way legislation might go to act hastily.

For example, have we adequately considered the meaning of autonomy? How does it operate in a social context? Does it have its limits? Have we sufficiently thought through the probable and possible consequences, good and bad, of both allowing and disallowing these measures? Can the problems contributing to a desire for euthanasia be remedied by other means? Have all reasonable alternatives been tried? Could it be that legalized euthanasia will leave unresolved the root problems associated with care of the terminally ill and dying, and deal with only the symptoms? How would a policy of legalized euthanasia be reconciled with basic moral convictions as well as with the beliefs of most religious traditions? Many such considerations deserve to be thought through before we try to "settle" the issue through legislation.

Furthermore, efforts at legislation right now could well precipitate a polarization in society similar to what we've experienced in the abortion controversy. In a sense we're all on the same side on this issue—we do want to make dying as humane as possible. We can share at least this common goal. But people differ on how to achieve that goal. Legislation will likely force an either/or option. Perhaps with more discussion, increased understanding, and some honest and cooperative dialogue, some of the polarization can be avoided. We should have learned from debates over abortion that in these situations it is hard to resolve anything more than issues of power. We should also have learned that emotional events (like the Kevorkian and Cruzan cases) and emotional causes (which this quite likely is) can lead people who waver and people in the middle to choose a side. When that happens, many stop listening, stop discussing, stop thinking. We must try to avoid that.

22. So we do nothing? That leads to chaos, doesn't it?

Doing nothing on the legislative front, some advisors say, would be better than doing everything or trying too much at this time. It is probably safe to say that if you brought together the most seasoned and respected ethicists and the most experienced medical, legal, and clergy personnel, their general counsel would be "go slowly!" Too many other things have to happen. And they would probably give the same caution to legislators: Take your time. Resist stampedes. Don't let interest groups pressure you into premature or sweeping decisions. Something will get lost along the way.

But doing nothing on the legislative front doesn't mean doing nothing at all. There are innumerable opportunities for public education, discussion, and eventually debate. Religious communities, health care and educational institutions, health-related organizations, professional societies, and senior citizens' organizations can all make a contribution here. Keeping people informed and involved is one of the most urgent tasks for churches and synagogues, hospitals that care about human relations, and universities with a public concern.

There is also the possibility of holding town meetings and open forums across the country. The more such meetings and forums occur, the more likely the public will equip itself to participate thoughtfully in addressing an issue in which it has so much at stake. At present, so many of us don't quite know what position to stand for, what outcomes to pursue, what laws to write, or even what beliefs to hold. Much could be gained by a period of listening and learning and by concerted efforts to address the treatment problems and the issues that euthanasia brings to the fore.

23. But isn't euthanasia ultimately an individual matter, a matter of personal choice, a decision among patient, physician, and family? Why get sidetracked with all these moral, religious, and legal debates?

True, euthanasia *is* a matter of personal choice. But it's not quite that simple. We are not merely a collection of isolated, self-determining individuals. We are social by nature; we are connected to others in many different ways. Because of that interconnectedness and the impact of individual acts of euthanasia upon those others, euthanasia is also a social issue and therefore a matter of public policy. It is utterly unrealistic to think that individuals can go about choosing euthanasia without its having some impact upon family members and friends, the various communities of which they are a part, and even society as a whole. These entities can be, are, and will be affected by instances of euthanasia. And in addition, it should be kept in mind that actions reflect and give expression to certain values and beliefs. The more people who perform a certain action and the more frequently they perform it, the more those values and beliefs get expressed. The effect is cumulative and eventually influences the moral tone or character of a society. Whether we like it or not, individual acts of euthanasia have consequences and implications beyond the individual decision-makers. As a result, we need to be concerned not only with individual welfare but also with societal welfare. For some, the struggle occurs at precisely this point. They believe euthanasia can be morally justified in certain individual cases, but they are gravely concerned about the possible consequences of a public policy of active voluntary euthanasia.

So present and future legal debates are not getting us sidetracked; they are at the heart of the matter because they deal with the social side of the issue. So are moral and religious considerations. Taking of human life, whether justified or not, is always of moral concern. And better to insist that any taking of life be justified than allow it to occur at anyone's whim. Though difficult, there is much to be gained from public moral argument. For those who are believers, there is no escaping the religious questions. They are there.

24. It seems that the euthanasia issue affects just about everyone and that everyone has a stake in how it's resolved.

That's true. Doctors, nurses, and hospital administrators, for example. Depending on what happens, they might be asked to participate in what might be either humane care or a betrayal of their profession and even a criminal act. They might respond with mercy to cries of pain or respond to charges that they are involved in homicide. Health care professionals can't afford not to care about this issue. They have at stake their responsibility to care for the terminally ill and dying as well as the very meaning of their profession.

25. What do others have at stake?

Well, clergy have much at stake. They help keep religious and moral traditions alive. They counsel families in times of agony and distress. If they stand in the way of loving acts in the name of laws claimed to be divine, they seem cruel. If they stand with those who want their pain and suffering ended and with those who are willing to end it, they may be accused of betraying their deepest beliefs, violating the divine will, and eroding respect for human life.

Lawyers and lawmakers are also affected. Take legislators: if they ignore this issue or oppose the legalization of euthanasia, they will be criticized by many as being ignorant or inhumane. If they support it, others will accuse them of undermining societal respect for life, of endorsing homicide, and the like.

26. What about the "person in the street"?

At a very basic level, everyone has much at stake. Anyone may someday encounter a loved one pleading for relief of pain and suffering. Even more fundamentally, everyone has to die, and everyone knows that today the many ways to prolong life can make the end of life something even more dreaded than it used to be. When people today talk about euthanasia, they are in some sense talking about themselves.

27. This personal angle does seem to make euthanasia a special issue.

There *is* something distinctive about it. In fact, this feature sets it apart from the other most troubling medical ethics issue in our society—abortion. While abortion involves the personhood, autonomy, meaning, and agency of a particular mother, legislators and hospital administrators, to say nothing of interest groups, more readily talk about abortion in broad, inclusive, abstract, and impersonal ways. Not so with euthanasia. The talk is about Adkins or Cruzan, or a friend or a relative or a spouse, or one's very self!

It may be good that whenever we talk about euthanasia we get to very specific cases, with people who have names, whose life stories have to be understood. Each of us can *become* such a case, and all of us are living out such stories. That is why we read ourselves into others' narratives, whether positively ("I could see myself doing that") or negatively ("What a horrible thing for anyone to do. I wouldn't!").

Some ethical issues in health care attract only elites and experts. *My* living and dying, *my* life story finds no one more concerned than I am. It's partly for this reason that the public is becoming more and more informed and involved.

28. It does seem as though euthanasia is everyone's issue. With everyone having a stake in the matter, it only makes sense that everyone's voice should be heard.

Well, that's true. In particular we probably need to be attentive to the experience and the insights of those who are living through the kinds of pain and suffering that give rise to requests for euthanasia—the terminally ill, the dying, and the elderly who are overwhelmed with the debilitating burdens associated with aging. The family members and intimate friends who accompany these individuals through their ordeals also should be listened to with great care. Then, of course, we should hear from the physicians and nurses who see illness and suffering firsthand and try their best to remedy or alleviate it within the limits of their own professional belief systems and commitments. The insight and wisdom based on their experiences will be invaluable.

Others, too, have indispensable contributions to make from the perspective of their own life stories and their professional engagements. Lawmakers are likely to call our attention to what is good for society as a whole. Their primary interest will be with developing a viable public policy. Clergy will likely attempt to keep the resources of their religious traditions in the forefront of the debate and draw out the implications and the wisdom of those traditions for the members of their believing communities.

Philosophers and theologians have different professional concerns and their own contribution to make. They raise and try to answer life's basic questions: what is the meaning of life and death, of pain and suffering, of human finitude, of illness and aging, of healing and health? They will draw upon human experience as well as a variety of philosophical and religious traditions and struggle with the moral justifiability of assisted suicide and active euthanasia. While their contributions may at times seem somewhat abstract and unrelated to John Doe who is dying of AIDS or Mary Smith who is suffering from advanced Alzheimer's, they ultimately are not. All people bring to these issues their own fundamental beliefs—their own answers to life's basic questions. Philosophers and theologians help us to become aware of them, to understand them, and perhaps to revise them. They also help us to clarify our reasons for holding the positions we hold and offer for our consideration alternative perspectives and arguments.

Many have something to say about this issue, and many perspectives need to be considered. This is why assisted suicide and active euthanasia deserve a full airing before we decide on practice or policy.

It is toward this end that we have prepared these materials. They are meant as an introduction to the discussion. They are also meant to call attention to the various traditions we each inherit and inhabit but often do not think about until we are confronted with trying situations that raise life's basic questions. These situations often direct us back to our roots to rediscover "who we are" and to find in our traditions resources for meaning, resources ultimately for living and, yes, dying.

Martin E. Marty
Ron P. Hamel

4

VIEWS OF THE
MAJOR FAITH TRADITIONS

The attitudes of various religious bodies toward active euthanasia are central to any discussion of the morality and legalization of euthanasia. For this reason, we present here the thinking of a number of major faith traditions. Active euthanasia has been our primary focus, but we have also included, when these existed and were available, denominational positions on forgoing life-sustaining treatment.

Each presentation is prefaced by a brief treatment of the tradition or denomination as well as of the authoritative weight and binding force of its position on euthanasia.[1] Needless to say, this authority varies widely among the various religious groups. The teachings of some traditions with regard to euthanasia are prescriptive; of others, instructive. In some traditions, members are to obey, while in others, members are to be guided by their consciences. Many denominations do not have anything resembling an "official" position. Some have not given any specific attention to active euthanasia. Others expect to take it up in the near future.

For accuracy, and to make the position statements accessible to our readers, we have whenever possible included large portions of the statements themselves. We have made every effort to be precise and fair within the limits of our resources and the cooperation of representatives of the various religious groups.

Western Religious Traditions

Judaism

The history of the Jewish tradition reaches back to Abraham, but it is particularly the Exodus-Sinai events that constituted the ancient Hebrews as a people. Their earliest history is to be found in the Torah, Prophets, and Writings, which are known as the Hebrew Bible. Much of Jewish history is characterized by persecution, conquest, and exile. This accounts to a considerable degree for Judaism's spread over the centuries across the Mediterranean region and to eastern and western Europe.

Jews arrived in the United States in the early days of the American colonies. The first official congregation was established in North America in 1654 in Peter Stuyvesant's New Amsterdam. There are now four divisions in American Judaism—Orthodox, Conservative, Reconstructionist, and Reform. Congregations, each headed up by a rabbi, enjoy full independence. Moral guidance is provided by the study of halakha, the Jewish system of law and ethics. The sources of halakha include the Torah and the Talmud. There are no central governing bodies.

Judaism's basic religious document is the Torah, the first five books of the Hebrew scriptures, which contain the earliest written traditions and laws of the Jewish people. The Torah is considered divine revelation and is the basic constitution of the Jewish people.

A second, encyclopedic body of literature, the Talmud, consists of rabbinic interpretations and annotations on the Mishnah—the first authoritative codification of Jewish oral law—and on other collections of oral law. This collection of law, lore, and commentary was produced by two groups of Jewish scholars, one in Palestine, completing its work around 400 C.E., and the other in Babylon, finishing about a century later. For the Orthodox and Conservative traditions, the rabbinical literature is considered coequal in divine authority to the Torah. This rabbinic literature, especially the Babylonian Talmud, is the primary source of Jewish teaching in general and of Jewish medical ethics in particular.

The final redaction of the Talmud did not signal the end of halakhic discussion. During the Middle Ages, there appeared two genres of legal literature—responsa and codes. The responsa literature is the compilation of answers by individual rabbis or groups of rabbis to questions from members of the community or from other rabbis on religious, legal, and social matters. From the eighth century on, one finds responsa on a vast variety of subjects. They came to be accepted as authoritative and were passed down to succeeding generations. They serve as the major sources of ongoing application of existing Jewish law to new situations. Any rabbi can issue a responsum, and there is no formal mechanism across the traditions in Judaism for resolving conflicting opinions or for determining the authoritative Jewish position. There is diversity among the various branches with regard to collecting and publishing the responsa.

The codes serve as a practical, summary statement of Jewish law. In addition to the Talmudic literature, the two most often cited sources are the twelfth-century *Mishneh Torah,* authored by Moses Maimonides (Moses ben Maimon, 1135–1204), and the *Shulhan 'arukh,* written by Joseph Caro (1488–1575) in the sixteenth century with notes by Moses Isserles. However, most Jewish attitudes toward health care issues are based on responsa rather than on codes.

Not to be overlooked is the importance of folk wisdom and practice in Judaism. Frequently the rabbis considered custom a source of binding law, and where there was no law, the tendency has been to follow customary practice.[2]

How, then, is Jewish law applied to questions of medical ethics? There is a spectrum of approaches depending largely on the degree of authority given to the various Jewish sources. Orthodox Jews, for example, view the classical texts as completely determinative. They believe the Torah to be the literal word of God and the rabbinic literature to have equal authority.

Conservative Jews maintain that the classical sources need to be understood in their historical context. While they consider Jewish law to be binding, they believe that its content is subject to some change in response to different cultural and historical situations as well as to the challenges of modern life. Reform and Reconstructionist Jews do not consider Jewish law to be the authoritative word of God or as binding, though some may choose to use it as a resource in making decisions. For Reform Jews, autonomy is an extremely important value in the decision-making process.[3]

Despite these differences in the weight given to classical sources, there does appear to be a consensus among the majority of rabbis from all four branches of Judaism that active euthanasia is not morally justified. This position is grounded in both the Torah and rabbinic sources.

With regard to the biblical texts, Fred Rosner writes:

> In the book of Genesis, 9:6, we find: "Whoso sheddeth man's blood, by man shall his blood be shed. . . ." In the second book of the Pentateuch, Exodus 21:14, is the following sentence: "And if a man come presumptuously upon his neighbor, to slay him with guile: thou shalt take him from Mine altar, that he may die." In Leviticus 24:17, is the phrase "And he that smiteth any man mortally shall surely be put to death" and four sentences later we find again ". . . And he that killeth a man shall be put to death." In the book of Numbers it is stated (35:30): "Whoso killeth any person, the murderer shall be slain at the mouth of witnesses" Finally in Deuteronomy, the sixth commandment of the decalogue is repeated (5:17): "Thou shalt not murder." Thus, in every book of the Pentateuch, we find at least one reference to murder or killing.[4]

In the Mishnah, one finds the following (Shemahot 1:4):

> "One may not close the eyes of the dying person. He who touches them or moves them is shedding blood because Rabbi Meir used to say: this can be compared to a flickering flame. As soon as a person touches it, it becomes extinguished. So too, whosoever closes the eyes of the dying is considered to have taken his soul."[5]

One finds a similar statement in the Babylonian Talmud (Shabbat 151b):

> "He who closes the eyes of a dying person while the soul is departing is a murderer. This may be compared to a lamp that is going out. If a man places his finger upon it, it is immediately extinguished."[6]

The code of Maimonides (Judges, Laws of Mourning 4:5) handles the matter this way:

> "One who is in a dying condition is regarded as a living person in all respects. It is not permitted to bind his jaws, to stop up the organs of the lower extremities, or to place metallic or cooling vessels upon his navel in order to prevent swelling. He is not to be rubbed or washed, nor is sand or salt to be put upon him until he expires. He who touches him is guilty of shedding blood. To what may he be compared? To a flickering flame, which is extinguished as soon as one touches it. Whoever closes the eyes of the dying while the soul is about to depart is shedding blood."[7]

The sixteenth century code of Jewish law by Rabbi Joseph Caro, the *Shulhan Arukh*, devotes an entire chapter (*Yoreh De'ah*, 339) to laws concerning the dying person. Like the Mishnah and Maimonides, Caro considers the *goses* (a term referring to the individual for whom death is imminent) to be a living person and prohibits a number of actions that might hasten the person's death, including removing a pillow from under the individual's head.

This prohibition of any hastening of death is echoed by contemporary Jewish scholars among whom is Rabbi Immanuel Jakobovits. In his book *Jewish Medical Ethics*, he writes:

> It is clear, then, that even when the patient is already known to be on his deathbed and close to the end, any form of *active euthanasia* is strictly prohibited. In fact, it is condemned as plain murder. In purely legal terms, this is borne out by the ruling that anyone who kills a dying person is liable to the death penalty as a common murderer. At the same time,

Jewish law sanctions, and perhaps even demands, the withdrawal of any factor—whether extraneous to the patient himself or not—which may artificially delay his demise in the final phase.[8]

A similar position is reflected in a 1980 Reform responsum to a question about the Jewish attitude toward euthanasia and the permissibility of terminating life-support systems on a terminal cancer patient in a deep coma:

> Jewish tradition makes a clear distinction between, on the one hand, positive steps which may hasten death, and on the other hand, avoiding matters which may hinder a peaceful end to life. It is clear from the Decalogue (Ex. 21:14; Deut. 5:17) that any kind of murder is prohibited. . . .
>
> We would *not* endorse any positive steps leading toward death. We would recommend pain-killing drugs which would ease the remaining days of a patient's life.
>
> We would *reject* any general endorsement of euthanasia, but where all "independent life" has ceased and where the above mentioned criteria of death have been met, further medical support systems need not be continued.[9]

Scholars from the various branches of Judaism echo the above themes in their *Compendium on Medical Ethics:*

> The Jewish attitude towards euthanasia as well as towards suicide, is based on the premise that "only He Who gives life may take it away." . . .
>
> For Judaism, human life is "created in the image of God." Although all life is considered to be God's creation and good, human life is related to God in a special way: It is sacred. The sanctity of human life prescribes that, in any situation short of self-defense or martyrdom, human life be treated as an end in itself. It may thus not be terminated or shortened because of considerations of the patient's convenience or usefulness, or even our sympathy with the suffering of the patient. Thus euthanasia may not be performed either in the interest of the patient or of anyone else. Even individual autonomy is secondary to the sanctity of human life and, therefore, a patient is not permitted to end

his or her life or be assisted in such suicide by anyone else, be he or she a health care professional, family member, friend, or bystander. In Judaism suicide and euthanasia are both forms of prohibited homicide. No human life is more or less sacred.[10]

Roman Catholicism

It is somewhat difficult to date the beginnings of Roman Catholicism. Undoubtedly, it originates with Jesus of Nazareth and the earliest days of Christianity, but its identity and structure as they are known today developed gradually. By the fifth century, however, it is generally recognized that Rome had become the ecclesiastical center in the West and its bishop the principal authority.

The church's polity is episcopal and hierarchical and is probably the most centralized of religious bodies. Bishops are the ruling authorities in their own diocese, overseeing individual parishes served by one or more clergy, but they are subject to the Pope, who has primacy among the bishops. The Pope is the supreme authority in matters of faith and morals. Papal teaching takes various forms (encyclicals, declarations, instructions, apostolic letters, sermons among them) each having different authority. Generally speaking, however, papal teaching on matters of faith and morals is considered binding upon Catholics.

The Roman Catholic church is the largest single church in the United States and was one of the first to be established in the country. Spanish priests accompanied Columbus in 1492, and the first parish was established in St. Augustine, Florida, in 1565.

The Roman Catholic church has a long history of theological reflection on matters relating to death and dying. That tradition reflects a consistent opposition to the direct ending of human life whether at the beginning or at the end, though it was probably the earliest proponent of the moral justifiability of forgoing various forms of life-sustaining treatment. As early as the sixteenth century, Roman Catholic theologians argued that there is no moral necessity to employ measures that are of little or no benefit to the patient or that result in a disproportion of burdens to benefits. This position has continued to develop over the years and was affirmed by Pope Pius XII in a November 24, 1957, address on "The Prolongation of Life."

The most recent authoritative statement of the official church is the Sacred Congregation for the Doctrine of the Faith's 1980 *Declaration on Euthanasia*, issued with the approval of Pope John Paul II. While this document does not have the weight of an encyclical, it is considered to be morally binding on Catholics. Regarding euthanasia, the document states:

> Human life is the basis of all goods, and is the necessary source and condition of every human activity and of all society. Most people regard life as something sacred and hold that no one may dispose of it at will, but believers see in life something greater, namely a gift of God's love, which they are called upon to preserve and make fruitful. And it is this latter consideration that gives rise to the following consequences:
>
> 1. No one can make an attempt on the life of an innocent person without opposing God's love for that person, without violating a fundamental right, and therefore without committing a crime of the utmost gravity.
>
> 2. Everyone has the duty to lead his or her life in accordance with God's plan. That life is entrusted to the individual as a good that must bear fruit already here on earth, but that finds its full perfection only in eternal life.
>
> 3. Intentionally causing one's own death, or suicide, is therefore equally as wrong as murder; such an action on the part of a person is to be considered as a rejection of God's sovereignty and loving plan. Furthermore, suicide is also often a refusal of love for self, the denial of the natural instinct to live, a flight from the duties of justice and charity owed to one's neighbor, to various communities, or to the whole of society—although, as is generally recognized, at times there are psychological factors present that can diminish responsibility or even completely remove it.

. . . .

By euthanasia is understood an action or an omission which of itself or by intention causes death, in order that all suffering may in this way be eliminated. Euthanasia's terms of reference, therefore, are to be found in the intention of the will and in the methods used.

It is necessary to state firmly once more that nothing and no one can in any way permit the killing of an innocent human being, whether a fetus or an embryo, an infant or an adult, an old person, or one suffering from an incurable disease, or a person who is dying. Furthermore, no one is permitted to ask for this act of killing, either for himself or herself or for another person entrusted to his or her care, nor can he or she consent to it, either explicitly or implicitly. Nor can any authority legitimately recommend or permit such an action. For it is a question of the violation of the divine law, an offense against the dignity of the human person, a crime against life, and an attack on humanity.

On the matter of termination of treatment, the document states:

It is also permitted, with the patient's consent, to interrupt these means, where the results fall short of expectations. But for such a decision to be made, account will have to be taken of the reasonable wishes of the patient and the patient's family, as also of the advice of the doctors who are specially competent in the matter. The latter may in particular judge that the investment in instruments and personnel is disproportionate to the results foreseen; they may also judge that the techniques applied impose on the patient strain or suffering out of proportion with the benefits which he or she may gain from such techniques.

It is also permissible to make do with the normal means that medicine can offer. Therefore one cannot impose on anyone the obligation to have recourse to a technique which is already in use but which carries a risk or is burdensome. Such a refusal is not the equivalent of suicide; on the contrary, it should be considered as an acceptance of the human condition, or a wish to avoid the application of a medical procedure disproportionate to the results that can be expected, or a desire not to impose excessive expense on the family or the community.

CHOOSING DEATH

When inevitable death is imminent in spite of the means used, it is permitted in conscience to take the decision to refuse forms of treatment that would only secure a precarious and burdensome prolongation of life, so long as the normal care due to the sick person in similar cases is not interrupted. In such cases the doctor has no reason to reproach himself with failing to help the person in danger.

Islam

Islam claims approximately six million adherents in the United States. Promulgated by Muhammad (570–632 C.E.), it is the last of the Semitic religions and claims to be the continuation of all former religious principles decreed by God through his revelations to the prophets. These include Jesus and many of the Jewish prophets and leaders appearing in the Hebrew Scriptures. The Islamic core creed is that there is no deity worthy of worship except Allah.

The authoritative sources of Islamic doctrine and practice are the Qur'an and the Sunna. The Qur'an consists of Allah's revelations to the Prophet Muhammad (considered the Messenger of God) and is the basis for Muslim law and theology as well as for the principles and institutions of public life. The term *sunna* means an example for others to follow. Hence, the Sunna of the Prophet consists of precepts and actions of the Prophet Muhammad not found in the Qur'an. Islam has no priesthood or organized hierarchy. The Qur'an, the holy city of Mecca, and the Prophet Muhammad are the mainsprings of unity.

Abdu Rsaman Bin-Salin, professor of Islamic law at the University of Medina, Saudi Arabia, has said that "euthanasia is 100 percent not accepted in Islam, for mercy reasons or anything." The support for this assertion comes primarily from the Qur'an and teachings attributed to the Prophet Muhammad. Several texts in the Qur'an can be cited against killing; for example, sura (chapter) 5, verse 3, is against murder, and sura 4, verse 29, prohibits suicide. The teachings of the Prophet state that killing is permissible in only three circumstances: (1) as punishment for adultery, (2) as punishment for killing someone else unjustly, (3) as punishment for forsaking Islam (and thus God) for no reason (for example, a soldier who deserts during a holy war). Otherwise, life is a gift of God and is to be protected.

Because Islam recognizes no intermediaries between humans and God, it has, strictly speaking, no clergy or hierarchical authority that applies across Islamic cultures. Muslims look primarily to the Qur'an for ethical guidance. As the revealed teachings of Allah, the Qur'an is intended to influence and provide guidance for human conduct.[11] The Qur'an constitutes a foundational resource for Muslim belief, values, and practices in all areas of life, including medicine.

Since God is the creator of everything (6:102), all pain and suffering is to remind humans of misdeeds in order to better the wrongdoer's attitude. When confronted with disease, pain, or suffering, the Muslim knows that God's will is somehow involved, whether directly by causing the condition or indirectly by allowing it to happen. Suffering and illness clearly show that the originally planned wholeness of creation has been disturbed either because God is punishing the wrongdoer or because humans must directly suffer the consequences of sin. Restoration to physical and spiritual wholeness lies in faith, piety, and submission to God's will. Mercy is not considered a permissible reason for killing. In Islamic thought, pain and suffering have a part in the reduction of sin. Therefore, to terminate suffering would interfere with the expiation of sin.

Similarly, the Muslim believes that death occurs in accordance with God's will. There is no direct and explicit text in the Qur'an on active euthanasia, but there are texts that prohibit the taking of Muslim life. "Do not kill yourselves" (4:29) has been taken to mean "do not kill each other," but it is also seen as an injunction against suicide, and in turn, is interpreted to mean that a Muslim killing another Muslim is tantamount to killing oneself. According to Islamic law, God is creator of life; therefore, a person does not "own" his or her life and hence cannot terminate it or ask another to take it. Since medical practice serves the will of God:

[The] doctor is well advised to realize his limit and not transgress it. If it is scientifically certain that life cannot be restored, then it is futile to diligently [maintain] the vegetative state of the patient by heroic means of animation or preserve him by deep-freezing or other artificial means. It is the process of life that the doctor aims to maintain and not the process of dying. In any case, the doctor shall not take a positive measure to terminate the patient's life."[12]

Protestant Denominations

Adventist (Seventh-day)

The Adventist tradition traces its origins back to the Millerite movement of the 1840s. At that time, William Miller (1782–1849) predicted, on the basis of his study of the Book of Daniel and Revelation, the Second Coming of Christ between 1843 and 1844. After the "great disappointment" of October 22, 1844, when Christ did not return, the movement splintered into several factions. The Seventh-day Adventists were one of these. Originally a small group, they survived to become the largest Adventist body in the U.S. and abroad.

The overall administrative body of the church is the executive committee of the general conference, which meets every five years. The committee is elected by conference delegates. The smallest administrative unit is the "local conference," of which there are some 413. Each has a great deal of autonomy and supervises all local and pastoral evangelistic work. Local congregations elect lay elders, deacons, and other officers.

According to the Health and Temperance Department of the General Conference of Seventh-day Adventists, no official position has been taken on active euthanasia. This is somewhat surprising given this body's concern for health and involvement in health care. A few references to the tradition's attitude toward euthanasia are found in writings of the denomination's ethicists. Jack Provensha of the Loma Linda University Center for Christian Bioethics, a physician and the denomination's first trained ethicist, wrote:

Personal life is precious as a gift of God and must not be rejected casually. The patient has the right to do what we may think is wrong but not the right to have others violate their moral standards in assisting her. Self-destruction is wrong whether assisted or not and whether compassionate or not. Compassion should be directed toward supportive care and pain control.[13]

David Larson, also an ethicist at Loma Linda, believes that an "informal consensus appears to exist among S.D.A. clinicians and theologians in favor of passive euthanasia [allowing to die] in at least some cases. The religious rationale is that it is both pointless and cruel to prolong the process of dying for no justifiable reasons."[14]

Baptist Churches

There are more than thirty Baptist denominations in the United States, reflecting a tradition of independence and theological diversity and a history marked by controversy and division. One of the most democratic religious bodies in America, Baptists emphasize the complete autonomy of the individual congregation as well as freedom of thought and expression. There is no central authority, though they do organize into local, state, and regional associations and hold national conventions to discuss common concerns and to facilitate the achievement of common goals. It is not surprising then that there is no "official" position of the Baptist churches regarding active voluntary euthanasia.

Southern Baptist Convention

The Southern Baptist Convention, organized in Georgia in 1845, is the largest of the Baptist denominations. It has no stated policy on euthanasia. However, the Christian Life Commission, an agency of the Southern Baptist Convention, actively opposes euthanasia. The commission espouses the fundamental conviction that "human life, from fertilization until natural death, is sacred and should be protected, not destroyed." Accordingly, "efforts shall be undertaken by the Christian Life Commission staff to oppose infanticide and active euthanasia, including efforts to discourage any designation of food and/or water as 'extraordinary' medical care for some patients."[15]

American Baptist Churches of the U.S.A.

The American Baptist Churches of the U.S.A., originally known as the Northern Baptist Convention and later as the American Baptist Convention, is the fourth-largest denomination. The body was formed in 1907, and its current name was adopted in 1972. The subject of active voluntary euthanasia has not yet been raised at a biennial meeting.

However, in 1989 the American Baptist Convention did issue a "statement of concern" entitled "Death and Dying: Responsibilities and Choices." It offers guidelines for choices that may need to be made about one's own or another's dying and outlines the responsibilities of the individual, the family, health care professionals, and the church in this regard.

The document is primarily concerned with decisions to forgo life-sustaining treatment "if no reasonable expectation exists for recovery." It encourages individuals to make their treatment wishes known beforehand (e.g., through living wills), in case they should find themselves in such circumstances. Families should be willing to assume responsibility for making difficult choices when patients are not able to and, as much as possible, to respect the previously expressed wishes of their loved ones. Health care professionals need to meet regularly to address all the issues relating to the care of the terminally ill and their families and to seek guidance from the families of patients whose wishes are not known. Finally, churches are encouraged to consider the issues addressed in the statement in the context of their worship, study, and care-giving ministries.

Other Baptist Churches

To our knowledge, none of the other large Baptist denominations—the National Baptist Convention of the U.S.A., the National Baptist Convention of America, the National Primitive

Baptist Convention, or the Baptist Bible Fellowship—has a formal position on active euthanasia. The General Association of General Baptists (a smaller denomination), however, does.

> We believe life and death belong in the hands of God. Regardless of circumstances that befall man, he must know that God gave him existence and He holds him responsible for his stewardship of life. . . . The deliberate termination of life is a serious concern, whether it be done by the person himself, a friend, or the physician. We oppose euthanasia, sometimes referred to as mercy killing.[16]

While opposing active euthanasia, this denomination does affirm the right of every person to die with dignity and rejects the pointless prolongation of a terminal illness.

Christian Church (Disciples of Christ)

The Disciples of Christ, which ranks among the dozen largest religious groups in the United States, was formed in 1832 out of a profound concern for Christian unity and a return to the beliefs and practices of New Testament Christianity. The church originated from the union of two movements. One was a Christian movement led by Barton Stone (1772–1844); the other was the Reforming Baptists led by Thomas Campbell (1763–1854) and his son, Alexander Campbell (1788–1866), all of whom had their roots in Presbyterianism. Alexander Campbell preferred the name Disciples of Christ, while the churches led by Stone opted for the name Christian Church. Regional, social, doctrinal, liturgical, and pastoral differences in the late nineteenth and early twentieth centuries resulted in divisions of the movement into conservative and liberal wings.

What is today known as the Christian Church (Disciples of Christ) represents the more liberal branch. Long a loosely bound association of local churches, the Disciples adopted a more centrally controlled and representative organizational structure at the 1968 annual assembly of the International Assembly. This, in effect, was a recognition that it had become another denomination. While the local congregation remained the basic unit, the churches were organized into 35 regions, each with its own boards and committees. A general assembly, consisting mostly of representatives from individual congregations and regions, meets every two years. In the interim, matters of church life are dealt with by a general board and its administrative committee.

By the 1970s, the restructured church began passing resolutions on moral issues at its General Assembly. This did not, however, diminish the church's long tradition of liberty of conscience. The *Handbook for Today's Disciples* (1981) notes: "If you ask about the moral correctness of having an abortion, the appropriate expression of human sexuality, seeking a divorce, consuming drugs or participating in any number of other activities which raise questions of an ethical or moral nature, the Christian Church (Disciples of Christ) will *not* provide a systematic blueprint for your personal behavior."[17] What accounts for this is the tradition of liberty: "While Disciples as a body may disapprove of the general practice of abortion, they recognize a greater danger of legislating a single moral opinion for all persons, thereby abridging the freedom of individual choice. On moral-ethical questions related to personal behavior, Disciples tend to affirm and reaffirm this position which is cherished as part of their heritage."[18]

The only action related to euthanasia taken by the Christian Church (Disciples of Christ) is resolution 7724, approved by the 1977 General Assembly. It called for a study of issues related to dying with dignity, development of a theological statement on this matter to assist members, and participation in public policy discussions to underscore the moral issues.

Christian Science

Christian Science was born in 1866 in Lynn, Massachusetts, when Mary Baker Eddy spontaneously recovered from a severe injury after reading the account of Christ's healing of the palsied man (Matthew 9:1–8). In time, her fledgling movement required organization and, in 1879 the Church of Christ, Scientist, was established in Boston. In 1892 the First Church of Christ, Scientist, was established as a worldwide organization.

The church is administered by a five-member board of directors in Boston, though local churches enjoy their own forms of democratic government. There are no clergy in Christian Science; services are conducted by two elected lay readers. "Practitioners" devote their time to healing through prayer. Generally, this religious body does not establish official denominational positions on social and personal issues. Church members are free to follow their consciences.

Christian Science belief in the power of God to heal, however, does have significant bearing on the matter of active euthanasia.

> Christian Scientists view the question of living and dying from a religious standpoint and rely on spiritual means for healing. They accept the fact that Jesus cured many diseases that were considered incurable and expected his followers to do the same.
>
> A Christian Scientist does not consider any disease beyond the power of God to heal. For this reason, he would not be an advocate of euthanasia. Christian Scientists realize the complexity of this issue within the context of ordinary medical practice, however. Also while Christian Scientists strive to follow Jesus' commands and to fulfill his promise of abundant life, they recognize, like all Christians, how far they still have to go in this regard. And they feel only the deepest compassion for those faced with the dilemma they may feel when struggling with pain and disease, either Christian Scientists or others.[19]

Episcopal Church

The Episcopal church is the American branch of the Anglican communion. Consequently, its beginning dates from a 1534 act of Parliament that established the supremacy of the crown over the church in England (and thereby renounced papal supremacy) and led to the development of the Anglican tradition. In 1789, after the American Revolution, the Church of

England in the colonies became an independent, self-governing body with its own constitution and American version of the Book of Common Prayer. The name Protestant Episcopal Church had been adopted in 1783.

The church's form of government consists of a federation of dioceses, each autonomous and under the administration of a bishop. There is also a diocesan legislative body made up of clergy and lay representatives from local congregations, and a standing committee of clergy and laity who serve as advisors to the bishop. Local congregations are overseen by a rector elected by the parish. Each parish is represented at an annual diocesan convention, and each diocese and missionary diocese is represented at a triennial General Convention. The General Convention has a bicameral legislature—a House of Bishops and a House of Clerical and Lay Deputies. Agreement of both is required to enact legislation. The Episcopal church requires unity in essentials of doctrine, discipline, and worship, but allows for considerable variation, individuality, and autonomy in nonessentials. Even official resolutions of the General Convention are not juridically binding on Episcopalians.

The Episcopal church has no "official" position on the subject of euthanasia. However, there was a resolution (B009) introduced into the House of Delegates in April 1988 requesting that the Joint Commission on Human Affairs and Health "study and report on the questions and concerns surrounding the right to die." It is not clear whether this study will include active euthanasia. The Officer for Social Welfare of the Episcopal Church Center in New York informed us that

> On all matters concerning health issues, Episcopalians are advised to contact a clergy person of their choice within the denomination to assure that both their medical and pastoral needs are met. . . .
>
> "Official" positions have not been taken because the circumstances involving decisions which involve the medical, spiritual and mental welfare of the patient differ!
>
> Guidelines for difficult decisions, i.e. abortion, euthanasia, and surrogate parenthood, are under discussion.

Timothy Sedgwick of Seabury Western Theological Seminary in Evanston, Illinois, and representatives from the Episcopal Church Center of Chicago both concur that there is strong support in the Episcopal tradition[20] that allows for the termination of extraordinary treatment but not for active euthanasia. A 1952 General Convention of the Episcopal church expresses complete "opposition to the legalizing of the practice of [active] Euthanasia, under any circumstances whatsoever." The reason given for this opposition is that the "Church believes that as God gives life so only through the operation of the laws of nature can life rightly be taken from human beings."

Again, it is important to note that even resolutions passed by the Episcopal General Convention are not binding on Episcopalians. It is reasonable, therefore, to assume that the positions mentioned above vary from believer to believer.

Jehovah's Witness

The origins of Jehovah's Witnesses' go back to 1879 when a Pittsburgh businessman, Charles Taze Russell (1852–1916), began publishing the magazine *Zion's Watch Tower and Herald of Christ's Presence*. Two years later he founded Zion's Watch Tower Bible and Tract Society, which was incorporated in 1884. In less than 10 years a small Bible study group had evolved into scores of congregations. They adopted the name Jehovah's Witness in 1931. Since the mid-1970s, a governing body composed of 18 members determines judicial and legislative matters by a two-thirds majority. All baptized members are considered ordained ministers, though only a fraction actually serve full time as administrators and pioneers (members who primarily witness and distribute literature).

Indications of Jehovah's Witness views on active euthanasia are to be found in their publication *Awake!* They reject active euthanasia for several reasons. First, it violates the commandment prohibiting murder (Exodus 20:13). Second, it violates the biblical command that Christians "hold a good conscience" (1 Peter 3:16). This phrase is interpreted to refer to the medical profession's general revulsion for taking active measures to hasten a patient's death. In taking such measures, one could not hold a good conscience. Finally, Christians are required to "be in subjection to superior authorities" (Romans 13:1) and to obey the laws of the land.

> In Jehovah's Witness thinking, active euthanasia is murder. Because they respect God's view of the sanctity of life, out of regard for their own consciences and in obedience to governmental laws, those desiring to conform their lives to Bible principles would never resort to positive euthanasia.[21]

Jehovah's Witnesses do not, however, oppose forgoing life-sustaining treatment in some instances.

> Where there is clear evidence that death is imminent and unavoidable, the Scriptures do not require that extraordinary (and perhaps costly) means be employed to stretch out the dying process. In such a case, allowing death to take its course uninhibited would not violate any law of God. However, there is need for caution before people decide that a patient is beyond all hope of recovery.[22]

Latter-day Saints (Mormon Church)

Founded in 1830 by Joseph Smith, the Church of Jesus Christ of Latter-day Saints has a rather complex organizational structure. It is based on the two priesthoods of the Old Testament, the higher priesthood of Melchizedek and the lesser priesthood of Aaron. The former holds power of presidency and authority over the offices of the church and includes patriarchs, high priests, seventies (Mormon elders ordained for missionary work), and elders. The latter has responsibility for the temporal affairs of the church and consists of bishops, priests, teachers, and deacons.

Three high priests—the Mormon president and two counselors—make up the presiding council of the church called the First Presidency. It has final and universal authority over both spiritual and temporal affairs. The president is considered to be the "mouthpiece of God," and the laws of the church come through him by direct revelation.

With regard to active euthanasia, the Mormon church maintains the following policy:

> A person who participates in euthanasia—deliberately putting to death a person suffering from incurable conditions or diseases—violates the commandments of God.[23]

Forgoing treatment, however, is a different matter. As with other Christian denominations, this is accepted under certain circumstances.

> When dying becomes inevitable, it should be looked upon as a blessing and a purposeful part of eternal existence. Members should not feel obligated to extend mortal life by means that are unreasonable. These judgments are best made by family members after receiving wise and competent medical advice and seeking divine guidance through prayer and fasting.[24]

Lutheran Churches
Missouri Synod

Founded in the state of Missouri in 1847, this second- largest Lutheran denomination in the United States is devoted to the maintenance of confessional Lutheranism. This allegiance contributed to a doctrinal controversy in the 1960s over the authority and interpretation of scripture, resulting in the exodus of over 100,000 members. It also prevented the Missouri Synod from participating in the merger of three other Lutheran denominations in the late 1980s. Decision making in the synod devolves on delegates to regional and national conventions. Triennial General Conventions of pastors and laypeople choose directors for the church body.

The Missouri Synod has been attending to the issue of active euthanasia for some time. As early as 1971, a resolution passed at the annual convention affirmed the church's belief that "human life is God's gift" and should therefore be "treasured, supported and protected." It went on to state, "We encourage all people to avoid perverting God's will by resorting to indiscriminate termination of life, either directly through such acts as abortion or euthanasia or indirectly . . . " (resolution 9-07).

A rather lengthy resolution, "To Affirm the Sacredness of Human Life," adopted at the 1977 convention, was specifically focused on euthanasia and provided the theological grounding for the church's position:

> WHEREAS, Life is a gift from God and comes into being by an act that shares in the creative powers of God Himself; and
>
> WHEREAS, Scripture teaches that suffering has a purposes [sic] of God; and
>
> WHEREAS, Life and death belong in the realm of God's providence; and
>
> WHEREAS, Scripture teaches that suffering has a positive purpose and value in God's economy and is not to be avoided at all costs (2 Cor. 1:5–7; 2 Cor. 4:7–11; Heb. 12:5–11; Rom. 8:16–18, 28, 35–39; Phil. 3:10; Col. 1:24); and
>
> WHEREAS, We sing of the positive purpose of suffering in our worship (TLH, 523, 528, 533, et al.); and
>
> WHEREAS, The Commission on Theology and Church Relations (CTCR) and its Social Concerns Committee (SCC) currently have a study in progress regarding the question of euthanasia; and
>
> WHEREAS, The willful taking of the life of one human being by another is contrary to the Word and will of God (Ex. 20:13); therefore be it
>
> RESOLVED, That the Synod affirm that human life is sacred and finds meaning and purpose in seeking and following

God's will, not in self-centered pleasure, a concern for convenience, or a desire for comfort; and be it further

RESOLVED, That the Synod affirm the positive benefits of suffering, so that God's children may be comforted in Christ Jesus and have their sights focused more firmly on eternal values; and be it further

RESOLVED, That the Synod unequivocally declare that the practice known as euthanasia, namely, inducing death, is contrary to God's Word and will and cannot be condoned or justified; and be it finally

RESOLVED, That the CTCR and its SCC be urged to complete their study as soon as possible.[25]

That study, known as the *Report on Euthanasia with Guiding Principles,* was published in October of 1979. It begins by distinguishing between active and passive euthanasia. *Active* is defined as "taking direct steps to end the life of persons who are not necessarily dying, but who, in the opinion of some, are better off dead" and as "the deliberate easing into death of a patient suffering from a painful and fatal disease." The commission does not agree with the use of the terms *passive* or *negative* euthanasia to refer to the discontinuation or withholding of extraordinary means of preserving life when there is no prospect of recovery. "This practice does not, in a proper medical sense, signify euthanasia. Instead, it normally belongs to the responsible care that medical personnel exhibit toward patients that appear to have irrevocably entered the process of dying."[26]

The term *passive euthanasia*, the commission suggests in the report, is more appropriately used to describe "the refusal . . . to use ordinary life-sustaining medical treatment" (p. 8). It constitutes "unjustified killing."

The commission, then, finds euthanasia in both its active and passive forms morally and theologically unacceptable. *"Euthanasia, in its proper sense, is a synonym for mercy killing, which involves suicide and/or murder. It is, therefore, contrary to God's Law"*

(P. 28). On the other hand, forgoing life-sustaining treatment in certain circumstances is acceptable.

> When the God-given powers of the body to sustain its own life can no longer function and doctors in their professional judgment conclude that there is no real hope for recovery even with life support instruments, a Christian may in good conscience "let nature take its course." . . . When the moment of no return has been reached, the discontinuance of what have been called extraordinary or heroic means for prolonging life is not normally a violation of God's Law. (P. 28)

The theological reasons for euthanasia's unacceptability noted by the commission in its report are threefold. The first has to do with the place of death in the *creation.*

> God created human beings to live and not to die. Death in any form is inimical to what God originally had in mind for His creation. Death is the last great enemy to be overcome by the power of the risen Lord (1 Cor. 15:26). To speak of "death with dignity" or "merciful release," therefore, consists of engaging in unholy rhetoric. Death entails destruction, separation and loss. None of these is part of the image in which God once created the human race (Gen. 1:26). Dying, therefore, is not just another point in the cosmic process or in the experience of living as it is often made out to be. Living is the only proper response on the part of a being created by the God of life. Death is the very negation of what God has given. . . . Death by every definition represents a defeat. (Pp. 18–19)

Death itself will be defeated "with the resurrection of the body to eternal life on the part of those who take God at His word" (P. 19). In the meantime, death is part of God's permissive will for the creation. And

> it is within God's purview alone to decide on the moment when the individual is to share that life which lies beyond death in a world restored to a splendor even greater than that of its pristine purity. Within the context of this certain

hope, mercy killing runs squarely against the grain of the will of a gracious Creator, who allows an alien power to fell man by way of death for the purpose of raising him up to the glory of eternal service and worship as a person belonging to a community of saints. (Pp. 19–20)

The second theological reason is rooted in the meaning of *redemption*. The Creator God redeemed the creation—overcame the gap between what is and what ought to be—by way of the suffering and death of his son. In achieving redemption in this way, Jesus Christ offers to all both a "paradigm for meaningful suffering" and an "opportunity to share in His suffering."

By such identification men and women can transcend the agony, pain and decrepitude which attend life and are usually the lot of those very individuals whom others might be tempted to exterminate by way of "death with dignity." The suffering endured by God's saints can be turned into personal Good Fridays. By virtue of Jesus' own suffering these dark days will turn into the Easter of glorification for all those who love God. Euthanasia, mercy killing, as a way out of such human hurt, may well be a way of circumventing or negating God's will for His children. After all, our Lord did not suffer in order that His followers might escape such an ordeal but that they might learn from Him what pain and illness mean by way of God's dealings with His children. (P. 20)

The third and final reason the commission offers for prohibiting active euthanasia has to do with the theological understanding of *sanctification*. The presence of the Spirit to the individual is immensely important for considerations of what it is that individuals might experience in that dim region between life and death.

In some instances it is impossible to determine by ordinary means whether the patient has the capability of reacting to what goes on around him. In such a situation it is of crucial importance to keep in mind that, in a patient's relationship to God, the Spirit has been given the special task of formulat-

ing and articulating "sighs too deep for words" (Rom. 8:26).
. . . Intentionally to bring about the death of an individual so
engaged in communion with the heavenly Father would
constitute a blasphemous intrusion into a sacred relationship prevailing quite beyond the farthest reaches of human
knowledge and personal awareness. (pp. 21–22)

The presence of the Spirit must also be taken into account
for a fuller appreciation of the possibilities available to the
patient suffering from those various limitations that attend old
age. Even an invalid, totally bedfast, can pray. "Such praying is
the activity of a life that is appreciated as being sacred because
it is intimately bound to God by His Spirit even when it is no
longer possible to say the desired words. Who, then, with any
feeling for the sanctity of life would want to cut short such holy
conversation?" (pp. 22, 23).

Furthermore, cases of lingering and even painful illness
provide to those who are well various opportunities for
demonstrating care (e.g., prayer, visitation). Suffering then
provides occasions for Christian witness and service.

The Social Concerns Committee concludes its report:

> Life as a gift from God is an endowment whose disposition
> lies in the hands of God Himself, working as Creator, Preser-
> ver, Savior and Sanctifier.
>
> Against this background the suggestion of deliberately
> accelerating death runs counter to what the biblical revela-
> tion offers by way of both moral principle and spiritual
> insight into man's nature and destiny as these are woven
> into the fabric of God's saving intent. This situation calls for
> increased acceptance of the disciplinary challenges inherent
> in personal suffering as well as of the opportunities for
> service to the ill and the dying. (P. 26)

Evangelical Lutheran Church in America

In 1988 the American Lutheran Church, the Lutheran Church in
America, and the Association of Evangelical Lutheran Churches
merged to form the Evangelical Lutheran Church in America
(ELCA). Until an ELCA general convention is held in 1992, the

newly formed church is relying on previous statements from the separate churches to represent its policy.

Lutheran Church in America

The Eleventh Biennial Convention of the Lutheran Church in America, held in September of 1982, adopted a rather far-ranging statement on "Death and Dying." Among the issues considered were theological convictions about death and the matter of active euthanasia. Regarding the latter, the statement distinguishes active euthanasia from withholding or withdrawing medical treatment, which is considered to be ethically justifiable in some cases. The same is not true, however, regarding euthanasia:

> Some might maintain that active euthanasia can represent an appropriate course of action if motivated by the desire to end suffering. Christian stewardship of life, however, mandates treasuring and preserving the life which God has given, be it our own life or the life of some other person. This view is supported by the affirmation that meaning and hope are possible in all of life's situations, even those involving great suffering. To depart from this view by performing active euthanasia, thereby deliberately destroying life created in the image of God, is contrary to Christian conscience.
>
> Whatever the circumstances, it must be remembered that the Christian commitment to caring community mandates reaching out to those in distress and sharing hope and meaning in life which might elicit a renewed commitment to living. (P. 6)

There is no further discussion of the theological arguments contributing to the prohibition of euthanasia beyond those suggested above—it is contrary to stewardship for the God-given gift of life and to Christian hope.

The document does, however, offer six "interpretive principles" intended to be useful in shaping responses to questions about death and dying. These presumably would have some bearing on the issue of euthanasia.

1. Life is a gift of God, to be received with thanksgiving.

2. The integrity of the life processes which God has created should be respected; both birth and death are part of these life processes.

3. Both living and dying should occur within a caring community.

4. A Christian perspective mandates respect for each person; such respect includes giving due recognition to each person's carefully considered preferences regarding treatment decisions.

5. Truthfulness and faithfulness in our relations with others are essential to the texture of human life.

6. Hope and meaning in life are possible even in times of suffering and adversity—a truth powerfully proclaimed in the resurrection faith of the church. (Pp. 2–3)

American Lutheran Church

The American Lutheran Church, in its report "Death and Dying," distinguishes between redemptive suffering and dehumanizing suffering:

> Christianity has long taught that suffering can have meaning. Through it God can work his grace for the one who suffers and for others. Redemptive suffering is meaningful pain. This is markedly different from the dehumanizing and mindless suffering of the artificially maintained terminally ill.[27]

This distinction and their assertion that "faith in Christ affirms the fact that his death and resurrection are meant for all persons on earth" leads them to sustain that "when death is judged to be certain and imminent, we affirm that grave injustice to the respect and memory of persons is rendered if extraordinary technology is applied." However, the report continues, active euthanasia is considered homicide and not morally justifiable:

> We affirm that direct intervention to aid the irremediably deteriorating and hopelessly ill person to a swifter death is wrong. While direct intervention in many cases may appear "humane," deliberate injection of drugs or other means of terminating life are acts of intentional homicide. This deliberate act is far removed from decisions which allow people to die—like shutting off a life-supporting machine or even withholding medication. Permission for the normal process is an act of omission in the spirit of kindness and love within limits of Christian charity and legal concerns. Direct intervention to cause death, known as direct euthanasia, cannot be permitted. We affirm there is a distinct moral difference between killing and allowing to die.

Mennonite Church

The Mennonite Church traces its beginnings to 1525 in Zurich, Switzerland. There its founder, Konrad Grebel, and several of his followers baptized one another because of their belief in adult baptism only. For this reason they were called Anabaptists (Rebaptizers). The name Mennonite came later from a converted Catholic priest—Menno Simons—who organized so many Anabaptist congregations that his name became identified with the movement. There are two groups of Mennonites, the Hut-

The local congregation is relatively autonomous and authoritative, though at times appeals are taken to district or state conferences. They also hold biennial general assemblies. Bishops (elders), ministers, and deacons constitute the elected officers of the church and exercise rather firm control over members' beliefs and behavior. Mennonites are known for their strong emphasis on obedience in following Christ, willingness to suffer for their faith (which many did), and a rigorous church discipline. They are also a "peace church," opposing military service and the use of violence.

While no formal position has been taken by the Mennonite church on either active euthanasia or terminating treatment, several sources seemed to confirm that it would approve of removing obstacles that impede a natural death but would not sanction active steps taken to hasten death. Erland Waltner, executive secretary of the Mennonite Medical Association, made the following comment regarding the permissibility of active euthanasia within the Mennonite tradition:

> No formal positions have been taken, but especially because Mennonites affirm that human life is a sacred trust from God and thus take a formal position against its destruction by active means, such as by war or by abortion, we would not approve participation in the hastening of the death process, though we accept death as a normal/natural process in human experience. Neither suicide nor active participation in suicide of a suffering patient would find general approval, though many would express a high level of compassion for those suffering . . . and would have a measure of "understanding" without approving "active euthanasia."[28]

United Methodist Church

The United Methodist Church, the largest Methodist body in the United States, resulted from the 1968 merger of the Methodist Church (itself formed by an earlier union of three bodies) and the Evangelical United Brethren. The Methodist tradition dates back to the late 1720s when John and Charles Wesley and a number of other students at Oxford formed a Holy Club meant to recapture the piety and intensity of the early church. It was established as an ecclesiastical organization in Baltimore in 1784.

Methodism is a highly organized religious body. The quadrennial General Conference, composed of bishops and lay representatives, is the lawmaking body of the church. Proposals adopted by the General Conference become Methodist law. Implementation is carried out by a variety of boards and agencies. Having said this, however, it is also important to note that the Methodist church has not developed an institutional tradition of reflection on the moral nature of specific medical interventions. That has been left to the theologians, though it is likely that there will increasingly be churchwide investigations and judgments with respect to particular technologies and procedures.

In 1980 the General Council adopted a statement on "Death With Dignity," but it dealt with forgoing treatment rather than active voluntary euthanasia. It read, in part, "We assert the right of every person to die in dignity, with loving personal care and without efforts to prolong terminal illnesses merely because the technology is available to do so."[29]

In 1986 the General Commission on Christian Unity and Interreligious Concerns of the United Methodist Church and the Bishop's Committee for Ecumenical and Interfaith Affairs of the National Conference of Catholic Bishops issued a common statement entitled *Holy Living and Holy Dying*. It was the result of the third round of dialogue between the two religious bodies.

The first part of the document consisted of a brief exposition of the theological and ethical principles that guide practice in various contexts. Those principles are familiar to the Christian tradition as a whole: human life as a gift of God; human responsibility for a stewardship of life; the fact of disease and death in the human condition; God's presence to human suffering and God's activity of turning suffering and death into wholeness and life; the Christian community's role in promoting health, in healing suffering, and in being present with the dying; ultimate union with God in the community of the risen Christ.

Both denominations accept forgoing life-sustaining treatment under certain circumstances.

> We affirm that the obligation to employ life-sustaining treatments ceases when the burdens (physical, emotional, financial, or social) for the patient and the caregivers exceed the benefits to the patient. The application of excessive procedures . . . does not reflect good stewardship because it does not serve the purpose for which God gave life. (P. 6)

They are divided, however, when it comes to the matter of active voluntary euthanasia. Some of the Methodists believed that under certain circumstances euthanasia "might be an ethically permissible action," but other participants, including the Roman Catholic team, insisted that euthanasia "is objectively sinful in any and all circumstances" (p. 13). Both groups, though, seemed unified in encouraging alternatives to euthanasia.

> The proper application of medical science, as demonstrated by hospice care, can in most cases enable patients to live and die without extreme physical suffering. Provided the intention is not to kill but to relieve pain, such methods of controlling pain, even when they risk or shorten life, can be used for terminally ill patients.
>
> If adequate support by community, family and competent pastoral caregivers is provided, the mental suffering of loneliness, fear and anguish, which is often more painful that physical suffering, can be alleviated. This support is particularly important in those patients who have very slight objective abnormalities or are without any physical pain but who suffer extreme emotional trauma in their knowledge that they are in the early stages of certain diseases: e.g., dementing illness such as Alzheimer's Disease, a slowly progressive but fatal central nervous disorder such as amyotrophic lateral sclerosis, or Huntington's chorea, HIV infection, and the early stages of certain cancers which with present medical knowledge are absolutely incurable. (P. 13)

This document reflects a theological effort and does not carry the weight of a statement coming from the General Conference, which to date has not issued a statement on active euthanasia. A resolution may come before the 1992 General Conference, but resolutions are generated by grass-roots efforts, so there is no certainty.

Reformed-Presbyterian

This particular family of Christians traces its origins to the Protestant Reformation but not in the vein of Luther or Wesley. Rather the tradition is based on the work of John Calvin, who established the Reformed Church in Geneva, Switzerland, in the

1540s. Calvinist-established churches on the continent were called "Reformed" churches, while those in the British Isles, especially Scotland, were called "Presbyterian." In the United States, the Reformed-Presbyterian tradition includes both Reformed and Presbyterian churches, along with Congregational churches. The latter, the church of the Puritans and Pilgrims, was the first of the Reformed tradition churches in this country.

What distinguishes Calvinists from other Christian sects is their "reformed" theology and the "presbyteral" form of government. The regional governing body of the church, composed of equal numbers of clergy (pastors and teachers) and laity (elders and deacons responsible for governance and the physical and spiritual care of the congregation), as well as the ruling body of each local church, is called a "presbytery." Several regional presbyteries (usually at least three) may form a synod, and synods may form larger bodies such as the General Assembly. In the United States, the latter meets annually.

In their 1983 General Assembly, the Presbyterian church adopted a statement entitled "The Covenant of Life and the Caring Community." The policy statement is prefaced by discussions of relevant biblical, theological, and ethical matters that also convey the church's stance toward euthanasia:

1. The direction of Biblical ethics is against taking the life of another even for benevolent reasons. Persons should not be deemed worthless, too old, too weak, unproductive, sociopathic or a burden, thereby justifying some act of positive "mercy killing," or the more fashionable slow killing by neglect. When persons fall into deep sickness, pain, suffering, unconsciousness; when they lie helpless under deep sedation or at the brink of danger in intensive care, they must know that they will not be abandoned.

While the direction of Biblical ethics is against taking the life of another, it in no way claims that it is necessary to prolong the life—or the dying process—of a person who is gravely ill with little or no hope for cure or remission. Persons who are terminally ill must be able to trust that their dying will not be prolonged by unrequested technological interventions. As theologian Paul Ramsey has stated, "We need . . . to discover the moral limits properly surrounding efforts to save life. We need to recover the meaning of only caring for the dying, and the justification—indeed the obligation—of intervening against many a medical intervention that is possible today." The existence of specific medical technology does not require that it be used. . . .

2. . . . In a pluralistic society where people have many different beliefs about life and death, basic Christian respect for persons demands that a person's decisions about death be honored in most instances.

The choice whether or not to undergo further treatment . . . should be a personal decision. . . .

5. The affirmation about eternal life that is woven into the Gospel according to John should be emphasized. Eternal life is here and now. According to the Apostle Paul, the light of promise shines in the present moment. That assurance keeps Christians from living all of life being afraid of death. Eternal life, not death, is the ultimate reality. For Christians the adventure is never toward an end but toward new beginnings . . . . For Christians, death can be understood as the next chapter in the surprising story of life. . . .

7. Finally, the Church is in the world to be an example, not to impose values or beliefs. By its life and its attitude toward life, it can and should bear witness to the faith. The Church in this area, as in many others, must be the community of care, protection and nurture. In this way, the Church can be a model in a pluralistic society for how these decisions ought to be made while preserving and enhancing human dignity and worth.[30]

This prefatory discussion was supplemented by several appendices including a living will, a document called "Directions for My Care, A Christian Affirmation of Life," and a "Form or Declaration Under the Voluntary Euthanasia Act of 1969." The first item of the latter form is a request for active euthanasia:

1. If I should at any time suffer from a serious physical illness or impairment reasonably thought in my case to be incurable and expected to cause me severe distress or render me incapable of rational existence, I request the administration

of euthanasia at a time or in circumstances to be indicated or specified by me or, if it is apparent that I have become incapable of giving directions, at the discretion of the physician in charge of my case.[31]

Thus it seems that while the Reformed tradition emphasizes the value God places on life and the respect that Christians should have for it, active euthanasia is not necessarily regarded as inconsistent with respect for life.

Unitarian Universalist Association

The Unitarian Universalist Association is the result of a 1961 consolidation of the Unitarian and Universalist churches in the United States. It is one of the most liberal and influential religious bodies in this country. The Unitarian church was formed from liberal Congregational churches; the Universalist church evolved from a variety of sources and has existed as a distinct church since 1790. The Association describes itself as a "free faith" church, that is, neither ministers, members, nor churches are required to subscribe to a particular creed. Individual freedom of belief, democratic principles, and the search for truth through the method of the sciences are emphasized. Both Unitarians and Universalists share a commitment to the universal principle of love of God and love to humankind, the supreme worth of every human personality, the use of the democratic method in human relationships, and striving for world community. Their constitution establishes a general assembly as the overall policy-making body for carrying out the purposes and objectives of the association. It generally meets annually.

The 1988 Unitarian Universalist General Assembly made the following affirmations in its statement on "The Right to Die with Dignity":

> Guided by our belief as Unitarian Universalists that human life has inherent dignity, which may be compromised when life is extended beyond the will or ability of a person to sustain that dignity; and believing that it is every person's inviolable right to determine in advance the course of action

to be taken in the event that there is no reasonable expectation of recovery from extreme physical or mental disability; and . . .

WHEREAS, prolongation [of life] may cause unnecessary suffering and/or loss of dignity while providing little or nothing of benefit to the individual; and . . .

WHEREAS, differences exist among people over religious, moral, and legal implications of administering aid in dying when an individual of sound mind has voluntarily asked for such aid; and

WHEREAS, obstacles exist within our society against providing support for an individual's declared wish to die; and
WHEREAS, many counselors, clergy, and health-care personnel value prolongation of life regardless of the quality of life or will to live;

THEREFORE BE IT RESOLVED: That the Unitarian Universalist Association calls upon its congregations and individual Unitarian Universalists to examine attitudes and practices in our society relative to the ending of life, as well as those in other countries and cultures; and

BE IT FURTHER RESOLVED: That Unitarian Universalists reaffirm their support for the Living Will, as declared in a 1978 resolution of the General Assembly, declare support for the Durable Power of Attorney for Health Care, and seek assurance that both instruments will be honored.

BE IT FURTHER RESOLVED: That Unitarian Universalists advocate the right to self-determination in dying, and the release from civil or criminal penalties of those who, under proper safeguards, act to honor the right of terminally ill patients to select the time of their own deaths; and

BE IT FURTHER RESOLVED: That Unitarian Universalists advocate safeguards against abuses by those who would hasten death contrary to an individual's desires; and

BE IT FINALLY RESOLVED: That Unitarian Universalists, acting through their congregations, memorial societies, and appropriate organizations, inform and petition legislators to support legislation that will create legal protection for the right to die with dignity, in accordance with one's own choice.[32]

This statement, along with the 1990 United Church of Christ Rocky Mountain Conference resolution (see below), constitutes one of the few denominational supports for euthanasia.

United Church of Christ

Four churches of major importance make up the United Church of Christ—the Congregational church, the Christian church, the Evangelical synod, and the Reformed church. They were united in 1961, though the first two and the second two had already previously merged.

Both congregationalism and presbyterianism characterize the organization and government of the United Church of Christ. The former is applicable to the local congregations, which are autonomous in their operations. The latter describes the churches as they are united. They are organized into associations (geographic groupings of local churches that meet annually), conferences (regional groupings of associations that meet annually), and the General Synod (which meets biennially). The synod is the top representative body of the church and is made up of delegates chosen by the conferences and ex officio delegates. The synod does not have the power to "invade" the local churches, associations, or conferences, but it does establish the various boards, commissions, and councils that oversee the work of the church as a whole.

To date, the General Synod of the United Church of Christ has not addressed the matter of active euthanasia. The Ninth General Synod (June 1973), however, did adopt a statement on "The Rights and Responsibilities of Christians Regarding Human Death," which focused primarily on forgoing life-sustaining treatment. It affirms that "nothing in Jewish or Christian traditions or in medical ethics presumes that a physician has a mandate to impose his or her wishes and skills upon patients for the sake of prolonging the length of their dying where those patients are diagnosed as terminally ill and do not wish the interventions of the physician."

The theological convictions underlying this position are set forth in the statement. First, "while we may and do learn from suffering, we do not believe it to be the intentional will of God that persons must be so tested." Second,

> informed by our Hebrew-Christian tradition, we affirm God as the source of all life. In creating us, He has endowed us with privileges as well as responsibilities; we are both creature and creator. . . . At the same time we recognize that our religious heritage has always stressed great reverence for human life as it is found beyond biological vitality. Thus the enhancement of life—responsible stewardship of our role as creator—requires equal regard for both body and spirit. Accordingly, overregard for the body, without proper concern for the needs of the person, or the human spirit, can become a kind of biological idolatry. What is required is a balanced appreciation of the whole person . . . . When illness takes away those abilities we associate with full personhood, leaving one so impaired that what is most valuable and precious is gone, we may well feel that the mere continuance of the body by machine or drugs is a violation of the person.

Third, "the Christian views death in the context of resurrection. . . . There is deep meaning in death, being the necessary experience through which one passes in order to experience the fulfillment of life that is eternal. . . . We affirm the meaning of death as the Christian's witness to faith in the resurrection of Jesus Christ."

The statement also endorses the use of living wills. "It is ethically and theologically proper for a person to wish to avoid artificial and/or painful prolongation of terminal illness and for him or her to execute a living will or similar document of instructions."

On June 27, 1979, the Twelfth General Synod reaffirmed the 1973 statement and adopted a resolution affirming its support of the legal recognition of living wills with appropriate safeguards.

In June 1990, however, the Rocky Mountain Conference—a regional body of the United Church of Christ—adopted a resolution, "The Rights and Responsibilities of Christians Regarding Human Death," which reflects a change in thinking. The resolution will go before the Eighteenth General Synod in the summer of 1991. The resolution reads as follows:

WHEREAS: We live in an era of complex biomedical technologies, with various means to maintain or prolong physical life and postpone inevitable death; and

WHEREAS: There are ever-increasing anxieties about a prolonged dying process with hopeless deterioration, and its potentially devastating effects on the dignity of the dying person, the emotional and physical well-being of families as well as the responsible Christian Stewardship of resources; and

WHEREAS: Technology advances more quickly than public policy, and public opinion often ahead of legislative enactment; and

WHEREAS: Individuals have increasing responsibilities in these life and death decisions, but often lack adequate information as to available options; and

WHEREAS: Life is sourced in God, and recognizes that our faith calls for commitment and work for the quality of human life with mercy, justice, and truth; and

WHEREAS: Affirming that the gift of abundant life is more than the avoidance of death and that over-regard for the body, without proper concern for the needs of the person or the human spirit, can become a kind of biological idolatry. We are convinced that what is required is a balanced appreciation of the whole person; and

WHEREAS: General Synod 12 of the United Church of Christ has supported the legal recognition of living wills and the General Synod 9 addressed the rights and responsibilities of Christians regarding human death; and

WHEREAS: We support the right and responsibility of individuals to choose their own destiny, and recognizing the need for safeguards to protect persons who cannot make life and death choices for themselves:

BE IT THEREFORE RESOLVED that the Church support the rights of individuals and families to make decisions regarding human death and dying;

Be it also resolved that the Churches within the Rocky Mountain Conference affirm the right of persons under hopeless and irreversible conditions to terminate their lives and emphasize that Christian understanding and compassion are appropriate with regard to suicide and euthanasia;

Be it also resolved that we call upon the Church to study and discuss these issues with resources provided by the Ministry Committee recognizing and respecting the rights of those who disagree;

Be it also resolved that we encourage legislation to safeguard all of these rights, including the rights of those who are unable to make decisions for themselves;

Be it also resolved that the Rocky Mountain Conference present this resolution to General Synod 18 . . . .

Eastern Religious Traditions

Eastern Orthodox

The Eastern Orthodox church is the result of the "great schism" between eastern and western Christianity that occurred in 1054 with the mutual excommunication of the pope of Rome and the patriarch of Constantinople. Cultural, political, liturgical, and doctrinal differences caused the schism.

The pope remained head of the Western church, but the Eastern church developed national autonomous sees organized around the office and person of the bishop. The more prominent sees were designated patriarchates. In addition to the four ancient patriarchates (Constantinople, Alexandria, Antioch, and Jerusalem), there are four modern patriarchates (Russia, Serbia, Romania, and Bulgaria), six self-governing (autocephalous) churches (Ukraine, Cypress, Albania, Greece, Poland, and Georgia), and six partially dependent (autonomous) churches (Finland, Estonia, Czechoslovakia, Latvia, Lithuania, and Mt. Sinai). The patriarchs have equal authority and have no jurisdiction in each other's see. They are, however, "in communion" with one another and are represented by the "ecumenical" patriarch of Constantinople. His position of primacy is one of honor only, and not of power. The Greek Orthodox and the Russian Orthodox are the two largest Eastern Orthodox churches in the United States.

Sources of Eastern Orthodox ethics are scripture and tradition, that is, the "mind of the church" as discerned in the decisions of ecumenical and local councils, the writings of the Fathers of the Church, and canon law. In other words, ethical judgments are rooted in the doctrine, liturgical life, ethical teaching, and law embedded in the church's history. Matters not dealt with in these ancient sources are taken up by modern Orthodox ethicists who seek to arrive at ethical judgments that are consistent with the "mind of the church." Their explorations are provisional and are always subject to episcopal, synodical, and general ecclesial review.

On the matter of euthanasia, there are no official decrees, but there are guidelines drawn from the tradition and current theological study which may provide assistance to the local parish priest. If further assistance is needed, the parish priest refers to the diocesan bishop.

Greek Orthodox

The Greek Orthodox church has a "fundamental bias towards the protection and conservation of life." Stanley Harakas, one of the foremost Greek Orthodox ethicists in the United States, writes:

> It should be emphasized, that nothing . . . permits or advocates the active taking of human life, even [during the experience of] terminal illness. A terminally ill person remains a person, within a family, part of the human race, a child of God. Active taking of a life in such a case continues to fly in the face of the moral bias for the protection and continuation of life whether it be done by another person, on his or her initiative, or on the initiative of the terminally ill person.[33]

This tradition, however, does allow for some cases of terminating ineffective life-prolonging treatment:

> In facing illness, we are obligated to use every method available to us to restore health. The principle that life is so precious that it is to be respected and cared for even when health cannot be fully restored should be protected and maintained as ethically valid.
>
> When, however, the major physical systems have broken down, and there does not seem to be any reasonable expectation that they can be restored, that is, when over-arching evidence supports a prognosis that the patient is terminally ill, the practitioner, the individual patient, the family and all others associated with the situation are not morally obligated, and ought not to feel obligated, to expend energy, time and resources in a misdirected effort to fend off death.[34]

Harakas writes in a similar vein in his book *Contemporary Moral Issues*. Here he identifies several basic ethical traditions in Orthodoxy that provide guidance in right-to-die matters.

> The first is that God is the author of life and that we have the responsibility to defend, protect and enhance life as a basis for living God's will. God is the giver of life, and "in his hand is the life of every living thing and the breath of all

mankind" (Job 12:10). To wrongfully take the life of an innocent person is murder and is condemned as a sin (Exodus 20:13).

On the other hand, "it is appointed that men die once" (Hebrews 9:27). Physical death is inevitable, yet it is something which comes normally *in spite* of our efforts to preserve life. There is something which rings of the barbaric in calls for the "elimination" of human life. That is why *the Orthodox Church completely and unalterably opposes euthanasia.* It is a fearful and dangerous "playing at God" by fallible human beings.[35]

Regarding the question of euthanasia, he writes:

The Orthodox Church has always taught that euthanasia constitutes the deliberate taking of human life, and as such is to be condemned as murder. Yet, rapid advances in modern technology and new means of maintaining life have created a need for an explanation and clarification of this position. . . .

A partial answer to this question is to be found in the Orthodox perspective on death. The fathers tell us that death is an unnatural wrenching of the soul from the body leading to the destruction of the psycho-somatic unity that constitutes the human person. Here man is a microcosm, uniting in himself the material and spiritual realms of God's creation. In addition, he bears the imprint of image and likeness to God, and in this resemblance, Adam, the first man, enjoyed immortality. But through the Fall man rejected God, the only source of authentic life, destroying the likeness and fracturing the image. He strove to make his own life apart from God and, thus, chose death.

Nevertheless, God did not desire that His creation remain in its fallen state, and in His great mercy, He sent His beloved Son into the world to transform and unite all things in Himself. By His Life, Death, and Resurrection, Christ Jesus restored the image and likeness in man to its original wholeness. All aspects of human existence were thereby transformed including death which through the Resurrection has become a passage into eternal life.

As a consequence, Christians should cherish their life on this earth as a most precious gift from God entrusted to them for a time, never forgetting that this life has been bought with a price and already been made new in Christ. At the same time, we must accept the inevitability of our physical death, not in despair, but with anticipation of that Last Day when we shall all be raised up in a transfigured flesh.

A further inference from this conception of life and death is that we do not deliberately contribute to the death of others. Therefore, euthanasia being a deliberate taking of human life, does not constitute a viable alternative for the Orthodox physician or patient.[36]

Summarizing the Orthodox church's position, he writes:

The Church, therefore, distinguishes between euthanasia and the withholding of extraordinary means to prolong life unable to sustain itself. It affirms the sanctity of human life and man's God-given responsibility to preserve life. But it rejects an attitude which disregards the inevitability of physical death. The only "good death" for the Orthodox Christian is the peaceful acceptance of the end of his or her earthly life with faith and trust in God and the promise of the Resurrection.[37]

Harakas also provides guidelines based on Orthodox tradition to assist in making other kinds of treatment decisions:

1. We have the responsibility, as a trust from God, to maintain, preserve and protect our own lives and those lives entrusted to us;

2. In case of illness, we are obligated to use every method available to us to restore health, both spiritual and medical;

3. Life is so precious and to be so respected that even when health cannot be fully restored, it should be protected and maintained;

4. When, however, the major physical systems have broken down, and there does not seem to be any reasonable expectation that they can be restored, Orthodox Christians may properly allow extraordinary mechanical devices to be removed.

5. . . . This action should never be confused with euthanasia, which brings to an end, deliberately and consciously, a life which is capable of maintaining itself with normal care. It is one thing to kill and murder; it is quite another to "allow the peaceful separation of soul and body."[38]

Russian Orthodox

Responding to a questionnaire on the moral permissibility of active euthanasia and terminating treatment within the Russian Orthodox tradition, the Very Reverend Archpriest A. Mileant of Protection of the Holy Virgin Russian Orthodox Church in Los Angeles made the following statement:

> We consider that human life is a gift of God, which no one has the right to forcibly take away; however, in our teaching it is not necessary to take "heroic" measures to prolong the life of a terminally ill patient; in this case we leave the decision to God who gives life and permits illness. . . . If a person is in great pain and requests to be allowed to die sooner (or his relatives so request), we do not consider it possible to accede to his request, because we believe that suffering is often sent by God for the remission of our sins and the salvation of our souls; so if God has sent someone pain which cannot be alleviated by normal means (painkiller shots, etc.), we must resign ourselves in the knowledge that this pain is necessary and inevitable.[39]

Hinduism

Hindu medical ethics are embedded in ancient and diverse medical and cultural traditions. Unlike Western countries, where technologies of modern medicine have fostered new concerns with the ethics of hastening death, medicine in India continues to be largely indigenous, and as such ethical concerns with euthanasia are more consistent with the classical and/or folk religious traditions. Since Hinduism has no universally accepted scripture or priestly hierarchy, the code of ethics for human conduct has always been flexible and subject to local interpretation.[40] Of particular importance, therefore, in a discussion of Hindu views on active voluntary euthanasia are the shared concepts of *dharma* and *karma*.

Although the diversity of Hinduism makes it difficult to formulate moral imperatives that are binding for all, the historical orientation of the people manifests itself in a great respect and concern for continuity and order epitomized by the concept of dharma, that which sustains and holds a people together individually and collectively.[41] Dharma is the law of morality or ethics; adherence to that law is an obligation through which believers secure well-being now and later, after death. It establishes moral norms and expectations for every aspect of life. One's actions, feelings, and attitudes toward death, for instance, are guided by the traditions and structures of dharma that have evolved through the centuries.

Central to the theory of rebirth and the causality of life, karma is fundamental to an understanding of Hindu attitudes toward active voluntary euthanasia. Dharma assigns actions or duties, and karma holds a person to them. Thus morality inherent in every human action has a potential for immediate or later reward or punishment. One cannot alter that which has already been done, but the present and future offer opportunities for modifying one's fate. By this logic, life events imply antecedent actions that can be played out over multiple lifetimes. Karmic laws are invoked generally when unforeseen and undesirable developments like grave illness or chronic disability occur. The pain and suffering of terminal illness, for example, are viewed as the consequences of past actions. How one faces illness, disability, or death will help determine the conditions of the next or future lives.

The ethical problems encountered at death are relatively simple. Death does produce anxieties in the dying, and feelings of sorrow and loss in the surviving, but for the various traditions within Hinduism, death is not the opposite of life—it is the opposite of birth. The two events simply mark a passage.[42] In time everyone must die when the body is worn out and when one has paid the accumulated debt of karma. What is mourned is an untimely or premature death, for the unsatisfied debt from a past life is carried over into the next life. Death may come as a relief from physical suffering that reduces quality of life, and one can take solace in the expectation of rebirth. Therefore, a person should be allowed to die peacefully, for artificially or mechanically sustained life is of little value. However, actively to cut short a life through medical intervention would be viewed as destructive of one's dharma by interrupting the working out of karma in the patient's life. Active euthanasia would produce negative karma for both the patient and the physician.

Western medical knowledge, technologies, and practices are well established in India's urban areas, although not accessible to much of the population. It remains to be seen how this approach to health care and the ethical concerns associated with it will square with the traditionally diverse Hinduism of the vast population.

Buddhism

Buddhism reflects a bewildering doctrinal, liturgical, and organizational diversity, largely the result of geographical diffusion and cultural adaptation. As the teachings of Siddhartha Gautama, the Buddha (ca. 563-ca. 483 B.C.E.) spread through India into Southeast and Central Asia, Tibet, China, Korea, and Japan, Buddhism developed into a number of movements, schools, and sects. As a result, it is not surprising that there is no official position regarding active voluntary euthanasia. In the midst of its variety, however, some common doctrinal features provide ethical guidance on euthanasia.

The final goal of Buddhism is enlightenment, the transforming and liberating insight into the nature of reality. In the quest for enlightenment, all Buddhists undergo threefold training in ethics, meditation, and wisdom. There is a substantial Buddhist literature dealing with ethical or moral issues within its many schools of thought. However, the fundamental basis of all Buddhist ethics is found in the 10 precepts or teachings about veracity, justice, and compassion, the first of which states that a Buddhist should refrain from destroying life.[43]

Along with this fundamental respect for life, two central concepts are essential to understanding active voluntary euthanasia from the Buddhist viewpoint, namely, rebirth and karma. According to the Buddhist doctrine of rebirth, one has had countless past lifetimes and faces countless future lives until *samsara* (the wheel of rebirth) is ended by enlightenment. Buddhist cosmology posits six realms of existence for sentient beings; karma determines the realm through which one transmigrates. Of these six realms, the most beneficial form is that of the human being. However, its attainment is the most difficult; thus it is highly prized and to be protected. Buddhism therefore upholds the sanctity of all human life regardless of the condition of that life.

The Buddhist doctrine of karma maintains a correlation between action and consequence. According to this doctrine, each person's condition, with its particular joys and sorrows, is nothing more or less than the results of his or her past actions, good or bad.[44] The main Buddhist teachings on karma are summarized in the following statement:

> The cause of suffering is said to be negative karma and delusion. In this case, karma refers to the actions that leave an imprint of an according nature upon the mind-stream. A negative action is defined simply as any action that has suffering as its result, and conversely a positive action as any action having happiness as its result. Both positive and negative actions leave karmic instincts on the mind, instincts that lie dormant within us until one day the appropriate conditions manifest to activate them. If the ripened instinct is positive, one experiences happiness; if negative, one experiences suffering. . . .
>
> [The] . . . karmic seeds that are placed on the mind at the time of an action will never lose their potency even in a hundred million lifetimes, but will lie dormant within the mind until one day when the conditions that activate them appear."[45]

The reference to suffering is important in the Buddhist view of illness. Of the Four Noble Truths spoken by the Buddha, the first is the truth of suffering. This truth points out that birth, sickness, old age, and death are inevitable realities facing all beings in the six realms of existence. In Buddhism, illness, death, and karma are inextricably linked. All illnesses have their origin in karma, which has its origins in ignorance about the nature of reality. In some lifetime, when the person achieves true understanding of that reality, karma will no longer be accrued, suffering will end, and rebirth will occur no more. A Buddhist would view arguments favoring active euthanasia or mercy killing as misguided, contributing to the perpetuation of karma and rebirth.

George Williams, general director of the Nichiren Shoshu Soka Gakkai of America (a sect within the Buddist tradition), made the following "unofficial" statement on euthanasia based on general Buddhist principles and philosophy:

Question: Buddhism expounds the sanctity of life. Suppose a loved one is suffering from unbearable pain and wants to end his life. Is it still against the Buddhist philosophy to allow that person to die?

Answer: Your attitude towards euthanasia depends on your definition of "life". If you think a person's life in this world is mere chance, you will naturally think that you can end the suffering of a loved one by ending his life. And you will regard it as an act of courage and compassion.

It is taught in Buddhism that a human life does not end by physical death but continues to exist throughout eternity, and that its karma, both good and bad, is carried with it into the future. From this, it follows that one's suffering does not end by physical death but that it vanishes only when one changes that karma for the better. Thus Buddhism provides the means to change one's bad karma.

The power to improve one's karma lies in one's own life. It is part of the Buddha nature that is inherent in all life. From the Buddhist viewpoint, all life is infinitely precious because it has the innate Buddha nature or the potential to achieve

Buddhahood. The purpose of Buddhist practice is to manifest this Buddha nature or the greatest potential of one's life.

Of course I agree that it is unbearable to see a loved one in extreme pain. In such a condition, that person feels he has no reason to live, so he wants to be allowed to die. The people close to him will think that they should allow his wish to be granted out of their own sense of compassion. But isn't this too materialistic a view of life? Moreover, the truth of life reveals that death is not the final solution to the problem of suffering. The people who cannot bear to see their loved one suffer from pain will be able to stop their own suffering by allowing the person to die, but the karma of suffering still exists within that person's life. The only possible solution is to infuse that person with the life-force to change his own karma for the better. . . .

If people start thinking that they have the right to perform acts of mercy killing, then there is the possibility for this to happen where it can be avoided. It is very easy to accept the idea of euthanasia when many people support it, and it is very difficult to deny it in the face of overwhelming opposition. However, we should find the answer to this problem by understanding what life is, not by mere sympathy.[46]

Thus a terminal illness represents the repayment of a karmic debt. If the complete evolution of the debt were to be disrupted by an active intervention on the part of a physician or someone else, it would need to be faced again in a future existence. Indeed, since human existence is so difficult to obtain, a person whose life was prematurely ended by euthanasia might have to endure the same ripening karma in a disadvantageous realm of existence. Thus it would be better to confront the results of one's past actions in the current lifetime with spiritual teachers, family, and health professionals to assist one. This emphasis on karma, however, does not exclude compassionate intervention to relieve pain (though avoiding lethal doses of medication) or sympathetic listening and counsel. On the contrary, the physician should relieve the patient of his or her suffering, but not interfere with the working out of the person's karmic life

100

pattern by mercy killing. For the terminally ill, Buddhism advocates hospice care, not euthanasia.[47]

Ron P. Hamel
Edwin R. DuBose

5

IS ACTIVE EUTHANASIA JUSTIFIABLE?

This report opens with four narratives that explicitly or implicitly raise the possibility of active voluntary euthanasia. Whether euthanasia may be judged as morally justifiable in such situations deserves greater attention. Presented here are reflections by six individuals with differing viewpoints who were asked this question: "In your judgment, is active euthanasia ever morally justified for patients who are terminally ill and who request, either orally or through a written directive, to have their lives ended?" Their reflections should offer perspectives that may lead to further thought and serve as a basis for discussion.

REFLECTION

Ronald E. Cranford, M.D.

In 1989, 12 physicians, including myself, published our views on death and dying in the *New England Journal of Medicine*.[1] In distinguishing between letting die by forgoing treatment as opposed to assisting suicide and performing active euthanasia, we strongly argued that there would be less need for assisted suicide and active euthanasia if physicians were more aggressive and humane in letting hopelessly ill patients die. For example, when a conscious patient is removed from a respirator, the patient should be given whatever dose of medication is necessary to relieve suffering, even if the drugs themselves cause a coma.

So one starting point in any discussion of active euthanasia is that U.S. physicians, by doing such a miserable job of caring for the dying, are driving people toward the more extreme measures of suicide and euthanasia. In my opinion, the extensive support for active euthanasia shown in recent polls of physicians and the general population does not relate so much to a desire for euthanasia but to the public's fear (in large part justified) that they will have no control over their own dying. People fear that they will become prisoners of an unthinking, uncaring medical technology applied by timid, fearful physicians who don't have the moral courage to do the right thing and who are much more concerned about the remote chance of legal liability than they are about doing what's best for the patient.

Even though the current debate on death and dying is two decades old, no meaningful social consensus has yet emerged on the important distinctions—descriptive and moral—among letting die, suicide, and active euthanasia. Until we better understand these distinctions, it is hard for people to know exactly what they are for or against. The futile attempt by conservatives to classify the legitimate withdrawal of artificial nutrition and hydration from hopelessly ill patients, like Nancy Cruzan from Missouri, as "euthanasia by omission" only confuses issues in the long run. It does exactly the opposite of what is intended by prolife forces; it drives people toward active euthanasia by reinforcing their fears of spending the last years of their life in mindless, degrading existence. It is ironic that the two groups most opposed to active euthanasia—the medical profession and the prolife movement—are the ones most responsible for this grass-roots movement toward active euthanasia.

Some prominent physician-ethicists have argued that active euthanasia is so inherently immoral that, like other immoral actions (slavery and incest), it should never even be discussed by "decent folk."[2] They are terribly wrong. The movement of the populace toward active euthanasia cannot be countered by silence or by simple opposition to active euthanasia; it must be fought by being for something—in this case, the humane care of the dying, genuine respect for patients' wishes, a commonsense approach to stopping treatment and ameliorating suffering, allowing families broad discretion in making life and death decisions for their loved ones (consider, for example, the tragic case of Rudy Linares in Chicago, who disconnected his comatose infant son from the respirator while holding the medical staff at bay with a gun)—and by relying less on legalism, vitalism, and absolutism.

The medical profession and society will surely lose this struggle against active euthanasia unless they recognize and encourage more acceptable alternatives. The softening of my position on active euthanasia over the years has not in any way been brought about by finding this practice more attractive but by my increasing frustration over current practices in the care of the dying.

Is active euthanasia ever morally justified in individual cases? Yes, I believe it is, but only in the most extraordinary circumstances. A conscious patient is hopelessly ill with a severe disabling condition, neurologic or otherwise, which greatly limits his or her quality of life, and has no chance for recovery. The patient is experiencing extreme suffering, either psychological or physical, and there is no alternative means adequately to alleviate this suffering. The patient makes a clear and unequivocal request to have his or her life ended, not necessarily because he or she doesn't want to live anymore but because the patient prefers death over life in this situation of unbearable suffering. This scenario would satisfy the minimal threshold for such a drastic action as active euthanasia. In this setting, the patient would not have to be terminally ill or imminently close to death. In fact, it would make less sense to justify euthanasia if the patient was imminently close to death. Imminent death would usually mean that the patient was so near death that he or she was dependent on medical treatment and life-support systems to maintain vital functions. In this case, the morally preferable course would be to sedate the patient as much as necessary to alleviate suffering (even to the point of coma) and then discontinue life-support systems and let the patient die of the underlying disease process. If, on the other hand, the patient was not close to death but could possibly live for months or years with great suffering, then the case for active euthanasia becomes stronger. Physical conditions such as intractable respiratory distress, diarrhea, itching, and vomiting are much more important criteria for justifying active euthanasia than just one form of suffering, physical pain. Physical pain can usually be controlled with the judicious use of pain medications, whereas other kinds of physical or psychological suffering can only be treated with medications to the point of coma or with active euthanasia.

My views on whether active euthanasia is justified in individual circumstances do not necessarily reflect my views on whether the practice of active euthanasia should be encouraged as a medical or social policy and whether it should be approved by the courts or legislatures. At the present time, my major objections to active euthanasia as a social or medical policy outweigh my support for the practice in individual circumstances. My objections to active euthanasia are many. Active euthanasia would not be necessary in most circumstances if there was more humane care of the dying. Cases of extreme and refractory suffering, if the patients were treated well, are uncommon, but they do occur. There are meaningful descriptive and moral distinctions between letting die and killing such that a line can and should be drawn between these two practices, and these lines should be more fully understood before we embark on any course of widespread active euthanasia or even physician-assisted suicide. The practice of active euthanasia would be a new role for physicians and could dramatically change—perhaps for the better, perhaps for the worse—the relationship between patients and physicians. There could also be more widespread abuse of active euthanasia, and it would be more difficult to establish procedural safeguards to minimize such abuses, especially in chronic care facilities.

I do not believe that active euthanasia or physician-assisted suicide is intrinsically immoral. I am much more concerned about abuses than I am of the practice itself.

But the sorry fact is that we are driving people toward an option that doesn't have to be—except in very unusual circumstances.

REFLECTION

Rabbi Joseph Edelheit

The 1990s will demand of us a critical and often painful reflection on what we mean by life and death. We have spent nearly a century caught between the paradoxical poles of unthinkable acts of genocide and uncontrollable population growth. We have participated culturally in acts of violence which make death a senseless void, and we have engaged in scientific discoveries and medical technologies that have added measurably to both the quality and quantity of life. Given those highly charged paradoxical polarities, it is not coincidental that during the final decade of this century, we need to ask, What do we mean by life and death? The specific question of whether active euthanasia can be morally justified goes to the very core of how we will eventually understand what we mean by life and death.

Answering this question *today* presupposes our willingness to answer it *differently* as our understanding changes. The many variables in this area will determine the still emerging parameters of our answer. As a congregational Reform rabbi, I am acutely aware that my interpretation of Jewish tradition does not represent a "universal" Jewish answer, and my involvement as an AIDS activist has also given me a distinct bias. With these caveats in mind, I would support active euthanasia and even some selected cases of physician-assisted suicides with the awareness and participation of the dying person and his or her family and closest friends. I make this statement fully aware that life is a unique divine gift.

Jewish tradition teaches us that life and death are not passive, but active categories. One of the most quoted passages from Hebrew scriptures is Deuteronomy 30:19, "I have set before you life and death, the blessing and the curse, therefore choose life that you may live—you and your seed." Lost in the translation from the Hebrew is the grammatical nuance, second person singular, for the imperative: choose life! *You*"as an individual"are required to choose life. Would Moses have used this dramatic peroration if there had been any indication that doctors, nurses, hospital administrators, nursing and convalescent home staffs, judges and lawyers could all choose for you? Within the biblical setting the definition of life was simple—breathing. We have long since passed that watershed of medical innocence. Were Moses speaking today, I pray he would charge us with a more relevant admonition—"Choose life . . . unless it is a machine!"

The key element of the question before us pertains to the assertive participation of the patients "who request to have their lives ended." Not only is there a public consensus—there is a strong indication that scripture allows us this final act of free will. Even if some choose to interpret the final act of dying to belong only to the divine giver of life, the human *has* control until it is wrested from him or her. The passion to control the destiny of others, even if morally justified and necessary, cannot be allowed to eclipse this foundational area of human dignity. To this end, we must continue to ask each other—what do we mean by life and death?

Hundreds of thousands are sick and dying, and millions will eventually die, from the pandemic of HIV/AIDS. This disease has forced us only now to begin to reckon with the profound link between sexuality and death. We have spent nearly 20 years in a national debate about abortion and choice—defending the rights of an unborn fetus and attempting to define when life begins. How curious that the lines separating "prochoice" and "prolife" cross and recross as the rhetoric becomes more sophisticated. The debates over abortion and euthanasia are already overlapping. How many people understand the words *prochoice* and *prolife* and what they really mean? As a society, we are morally derelict if we do not answer the question regarding active euthanasia, but can we answer it without knowing and understanding what we mean by life and death?

We must in my view be able humanely to support euthanasia requested by patients and surrogates, a goal that can be reached only by the difficult process of public conversation. Allow me to close with one final provocative question, intended to communicate the urgency of our conversation. An estimated 10,000 persons in America remain in persistent vegetative states and cannot die for various legal reasons. How can we justify this indignity to them and their families when we accept as nearly axiomatic the deaths of more than 20,000 persons—double the number of those in PVS—who will die in wanton acts of urban violence with handguns? We can't seem to legislate a means to allow those who have no life to die, nor can we legislate a means to allow those who have life to live.

REFLECTION

James F. Bresnahan, S.J., J.D., L.L.M, Ph.D.

The possibility of approving physician-assisted suicide has been advanced by Wanzer and 9 other of the 12 authors of a recent essay taking a second look at doctors' responsibility toward dying patients.[1] But this proposal is carefully hedged by agreement of all 12 authors that "if care is administered properly at the end of life, only the rare patient should be so distressed that he or she desires to commit suicide" (p. 847). All the detailed discussion of good care of the dying that precedes that statement and the proposal for assisted suicide in exceptional cases emphatically makes a point that I would insist upon. What I call "appropriate care of the dying," a studied, compassionate, affirmative response to the needs of a dying person by caregivers, is entirely feasible today. It does not involve initiating a new lethal process with the purpose of precipitating death. But, unhappily, such good care of the dying is still not the rule in medical care in our society, as these authors concede.[2]

It is my experience that the strongest motivation to seek assisted suicide or active euthanasia for oneself is a sadly well-founded fear that neither medical practice nor the law strongly enough favors discontinuing excessively burdensome medical treatment (so judged by each patient, one by one). A substantial minority of the medical profession does not recognize in practice the harmful impact of patently futile cure-oriented treatment of the dying. What those who fear uncontrolled use of medical technology are demanding, therefore, is authorization for a preemptive response to the dangers of cure-fanaticism and technologically elegant but humanly futile dike-plugging in modern medical practice.

At the same time, the hospice approach to a dying person[3] is denied standing as a legitimate alternative medical treatment. This is apparent even in the language of many court cases allowing the discontinuing of unwanted or futile treatment when by silence it is supposed that the alternative to so-called life-sustaining treatment is simply no treatment at all. Hospice medicine includes not only adequate and effective pain control but also, above all, personal communication and response to the dying person's needs. It includes as well the promise not to continue any kind of treatment that merely prolongs inevitable dying. But hospice is still all too often either openly despised or tacitly ignored as "not *real* medicine."

We must ask ourselves whether, as a society, we have become simply incapacitated from being sensible about when to stop treatments originally designed to help the survivable survive. We continue to use them to afflict the dying. Is the cruelty of prolonging dying a cruelty to which we have made ourselves simply unable to be sensitive? Are we so fearful of death that we can only recognize as legitimate and respectable "medical treatment" the kind that "prolongs life"? Is our only answer to take out a new kind of insurance against abuse—paradoxically in the form of authorization for precipitating death? This is just another way of not facing our problem.

It has recently been suggested that continued resistance to physician-assisted suicide and active euthanasia is due more to "moralism" than rational "morals" because it now frustrates the reasonable wishes of autonomous dying patients facing extraordinarily difficult situations.[4] Until we achieve routine appropriate care of the dying, I believe we are still missing the point, not being narrow-mindedly moralistic.

I believe that we in North America already find ourselves steadily losing our capacity to live and act in solidarity with the dying, including our capacity to accept and not hinder death when that is appropriate. The still widespread inability of medical practice to accept and deal courageously and compassionately with death manifests the progressive loss of our always fragile human capacity to deal with our *own* death and dying. Loss of this capacity is the source of the truly distorted clinical judgments of those physicians who cannot ever admit "my patient is dying" and act appropriately to ease suffering while letting death arrive. If proposals to allow active euthanasia are accepted, we will only discover a new way to evade basic and sane human realism about what human living that must end in dying means—limitedness and time constraint that we must come to terms with.[5]

In such proposals, too, we confront but another manifestation of our growing incapacity to recognize the demands of human solidarity, which can require sacrifice of individual autonomy to protect others from being brutally constrained to kill themselves or to ask others to kill them. As I see it, then, proposals to empower, legally and by moral affirmation, medically assisted suicide and doctor-effected active euthanasia can only lead to further distortion in our cultural inability to come to terms with death and dying. Far from being a reasonable response to legitimate requests for patient autonomy, such measures will make worse our disposition to take refuge from distressing human experience by seeking the deceptively easy technological "quick fix." This will be simply the ultimate triumph of technical virtuosity over humane medicine.

But what I most fear is that such proposals are being made

with a kind of insouciance about the violent character of our culture and our society. Already we have returned to the barbarism of the death penalty, and we disguise infliction of death as a benign medical treatment by using "lethal injection." In such proposals if finally accepted, I fear that we shall come face to face with the specter of our deeply hidden acceptance of violence—with psychologically hidden horrors that will take shapes we have not imagined in our worst nightmares. (And the suggestion that civilized use of procedural restraints on implementation of these proposals will protect us from the horrors of our psychocultural proneness to violence reveals a curious trust in procedure to overcome deep substantive deformity in our national character. In fact, procedures take on the cast of the substance they serve: if injustice, they become unjust, as the history of our constitutional struggles to deal with slavery and racial discrimination clearly reveals.)

We must cure our abusive medical treatment of the dying, and do that *first*. If we cannot do that, then we shall certainly have societal acceptance and legal authorization of assisted suicide and active euthanasia anyway—as the final expression of our obsessive denial of death, of our fear to come near those who are dying.

REFLECTION

Ronald Otremba, M.D.

Not morally justified

Is active euthanasia ever morally justified for patients who are terminally ill and who request either orally or through a written directive to have their lives ended? My answer to that question would have to be an unequivocal "no." Active euthanasia is never morally justified. On what basis do I make this decision? First, there is the principle that life itself is intrinsically valuable. This value is independent of one's physical or mental state of health. It is based on the principle that God is the sole creator of life and has sovereign authority over life and death. To some, this principle may seem cruel and unsympathetic, but it is, on the contrary, very respectful of the individual's needs and dignity. No matter what the condition of a person's life, there is still value in it. Value is not predicated on physical, emotional, economic, or social status but by the mere fact that one is human. This principle also gives us a reference for looking at two other principles related to the issue of active euthanasia—the principle of autonomy and the principle of burden/benefit.

The principle of autonomy states that the individual has a right to self-determination. This principle is not absolute but is subject to a higher authority or good. In application, the individual has the right to determine any treatment decision affecting his or her life. The individual patient has the right to request treatment, refuse treatment, or even terminate treatment once started.

Such autonomy is considered moral even if the decision means that one's life may be shortened by it. What is not moral is the decision to have one's life actively terminated. How does the decision to terminate treatment differ from the decision to end one's life when the outcomes are the same? In the first, death would most likely occur without treatment and possibly even in spite of treatment. It is possible to view the treatment as an intrusion or an undue burden in this case. In the second, the action itself can be viewed as a direct intrusion with the sole intent to end that person's life. There is a distinct difference between the two.

Just as autonomy has limits, so does burden/benefit. Treatment that would pose an undue burden on an individual does not have to be rendered. Treatment that has already been started can be stopped when it appears that the burden of the treatment outweighs the benefit that one hopes to achieve. It goes hand in hand with the individual's right to choose. The principle does not imply, however, that if life becomes burdensome, it can be terminated. Who determines when life becomes burdensome? The individual, the physician, society? What standards would be used if the individual were to choose? They would be totally subjective and relative to whatever circumstances the person found himself in. For one it might be a state of quadriplegia or the loss of a limb; for another it might be terminal illness, for another the loss of a loved one, and for still another, just the fear of being a burden. If active euthanasia were allowed on the basis of life's being unduly burdensome, each of the above circumstances could qualify; each could be considered so burdensome that death would seem a relief. Based on that reasoning, life would no longer have an intrinsic value but one subject to the changing tides of feelings and circumstances. If one were to have complete autonomy, one could choose to end one's life or to dictate that one's life be ended at any time and for whatever reason. Without limits, autonomy as well as burden/benefit would be subject to misuse and abuse in the form of relativism.

My obligation as a physician is, first and foremost, to practice within the guidelines of my faith and, second, to practice within the guidelines of my chosen profession. I am dedicated to the care of the total patient: to cure disease when possible, to alleviate pain and suffering as best I'm able, and to respect the dignity of the human person no matter how undignified his or her state of life may be.

Allowing active euthanasia, even though it be at the patient's request, would violate not only the principles of my faith but those of the practice of medicine as well.

REFLECTION

Karen Lebacqz, Ph.D.

Since the question to which we respond is already quite delimited, let me add one more condition: not only is the person terminally ill and requesting termination of life, but she is in enduring and intractable pain that cannot be relieved short of being under heavy and constant doses of drugs. Under these conditions, to ask the question whether active euthanasia is ever permissible seems to me a bit absurd, if not obscene. The question should be inverted: is it ever permissible *not* to use active euthanasia for one who suffers so, with no hope of recovery? We would not hesitate to put an animal out of its misery. Why, then, would we not extend the same compassion to a human being?

No, make that: the same compassion to our mother or father, our brother, our child, our friend.[1] Surely if we care about another, as Nel Noddings so forcefully asserts, we would want to prevent that other's suffering.[2]

Of course, there are all the *practical* reasons for not doing so. How do we ensure that the person truly requests euthanasia? How do we measure enduring and intractable pain? Who will effect the active euthanasia, and how can it be administered in a way that reduces or eliminates the likelihood of abuse of the system? These are not unimportant questions. But in my view, they do not undermine the central moral issue, which has to do with caring, compassion, and prevention of suffering in the face of death.

Consider a woman dying of bone cancer, the mother of one of my friends. As the disease progresses, the pain worsens. To handle the pain, she is drugged constantly and sleeps more than 20 hours out of each day. Is it better to be so drugged than to be dead? Is it different? There was a time when Catholic moral theology did not allow painkillers to be used during childbirth, ostensibly because of the importance of being in possession of one's faculties in order to face God.[3] While today we might deem the refusal of painkillers during childbirth rather cruel, the underlying principle of being in possession of one's faculties as one faces death merits attention. I am not sure that it is better to be alive and permanently in a drugged state than to be dead. Minimally, this seems to be something over which human beings should be given some choice.

I have watched my own parents sign "living wills" in order to try to retain some choice over their ends. Would I really have the courage to refuse treatment on their behalf if that came to be necessary? I'm not sure I would, for although I would want to honor their wishes, I would also have a hard time letting go of those whom I love so much. Would I then have the courage to give them something to induce death if they requested it? Would I be moved by compassion for their suffering or by revulsion at the idea that I bring about death? The questions are not easy.

Or consider my own case. My paternal grandmother died in a diabetic coma. A diabetic coma is perhaps a better way to die than some other ways, and it can be deliberately induced. Diabetes may be, in that sense, a "convenient" disease. I do not know yet whether I have inherited late-onset diabetes. If I have, I may have some options that are not open to those without convenient diseases. If my body were ravaged by disease, my spirit weary from intractable pain, my death inevitable, and my soul ready to face God, I would want to have something available to me to end my life.

That is not a decision I would make easily or lightly. I know the cautions about euthanasia—the danger that it is only a temporary depression speaking, and not the "real" person; the possibility that the patient to be killed is not in fact terminally ill; the risk that social policy supporting voluntary euthanasia would too easily turn into involuntary euthanasia. These dangers I take seriously. I belong to no organizations that advocate voluntary euthanasia, for I find them too unguarded about such dangers.

Nonetheless, I think there are circumstances in which active euthanasia is *morally* justifiable. To say it is morally justifiable is not to say that it should become social policy; that is another matter. Moreover, the situation posed here is very limited: circumstances in which patients are terminally ill and have requested that their lives be terminated, along with the further qualification that they are in enduring and intractable pain.

To sum up, I love life. I want my parents to live forever. I wish my grandmother had not died. I resist my own aging and movement toward death. And yet I am also a Christian. I know that death is not the last word, not the greatest evil. Failure to love, to care, to enact justice, to be in proper relationship—those are greater evils. Death can serve evil or it can serve the values of life. As a way of bringing about death, active euthanasia can serve evil or it can serve the values of life. When it serves the values of life, it can be morally justified.

REFLECTION

Stephen Sapp, Ph.D.

A wise old professor at my seminary used to warn his students of the danger of committing the "all or never" fallacy, meaning, of course, that few if any matters in human experience can be dealt with in absolute terms. I think that professor was right. Thus, although my general answer to the question under discussion is no, I am troubled by the inclusion of the word *ever*. Certainly one can imagine some situation where killing another person out of mercy might be morally justified. Whenever this question arises, for example, my mind often turns to the movie *The Great Waldo Pepper*, in which Waldo chooses—tragically but rightly, I think—to kill his best friend, who has manifested a lifelong horror of burning to death and is now trapped in a burning plane. Killing his friend is wrong, but it is understandable and certainly pardonable under the dire circumstances, and most of the time I hope I could display that same moral courage if I ever found myself in such a situation.

To build a general policy on such exceptional cases, however, seems to me dangerous. Institutionalizing the practice of active euthanasia will invariably lead to reducing the need for tremendous moral struggle in each instance, for wrestling with the awesome decision to take another human being's life. This reduction can only bode ill for our moral condition.

Our society, basing its view primarily on the fundamental values of Judaism and Christianity, has always forbidden the taking of innocent life and has considered that act one of the most serious, if not the most serious, breaches of morality possible. That one requests to be killed does not eliminate the very sound basis for that prohibition (leaving aside the significant question of whether such a request is genuinely voluntary, for all the reasons well known in the literature on this topic). There are more ways to violate a person than by violating his or her will, and even actions voluntarily consented to can still be wrong. The classic example is of course the voluntary selling of oneself into slavery, which is forbidden precisely because it precludes further exercise of one's autonomy. Certainly being killed, even if one requests it, shuts off even more completely any possibility of further choice.

What is distinctive about the situation we are considering that might allow us to set aside the age-old and almost universally accepted prohibition against taking the life of an innocent person, even if that person asks us to do so? Why are we willing *here* to kill people who make that request but not in other situations (for example, when someone has a gross disfigurement or is quadriplegic)? Presumably it is partly because these people are going to die soon anyway. *Soon* must be the operative word here because, as every instructor in death education courses is fond of springing on unsuspecting students the first day of class, we are *all* dying, yet most people are not considered legitimate candidates for euthanasia.

But how soon is soon enough? "Terminality" can be hard to pin down and quantify, and much good living can be done after such a prognosis. Suffering also enters in, as well it should, probably even more than temporal proximity to death. Any decent person hates to see another suffer. But again, how much suffering is enough to justify ending the life of the sufferer? Furthermore, many authorities suggest that much more can be done to control pain than is usually done now; indeed, permitting euthanasia may detract from the effort to discover more effective ways to manage pain, thus leading to even greater suffering for those who do not choose to be killed.

One group of special interest to me and for whom this issue has particular relevance is the elderly. Of any identifiable group in our society, the elderly are most likely to be seen as the "beneficiaries" of a policy that makes active euthanasia acceptable and readily available. Much has been written about the recent marginalization and devaluation of older people, their loss of meaningful roles and thus a sense of contributing to society, and their rapidly increasing numbers and their proportion in the total population. All these factors have led to calls that the elderly acknowledge their obligation to "get out of the way" so that younger, more productive people can have access to the resources the elderly are currently using. It is impossible to analyze the shortcomings of this position here, but we can hardly deny that our society's current treatment of old people destroys the self-worth of many and leads to their considerable guilt about merely continuing to be alive (witness the elderly suicide rate). Thus the truly *voluntary* nature of active euthanasia among the elderly seems hard to guarantee. The possibility of ending their lives sooner, with moral and legal sanction, may well lead to a form of subtle coercion, with the implication that the responsible course to pursue is to utilize this option. Advocates of active euthanasia, who see it as an expansion of individual autonomy, perhaps need to give more thought to this concern.

For some time we have been trying to solve the problem of aging by removing the aged from view. Now it appears we want to resolve the problem of suffering by removing the sufferer altogether. Is it mere coincidence that the two efforts are coming together in the push for active euthanasia of the terminally ill, given that such illnesses occur in the elderly in significantly higher proportion? The genuinely human (and certainly Christian) solution to the meaninglessness and isolation of old age— as well as that associated with terminal illness—is not to kill the old or ill person but to eliminate the meaninglessness and isolation through compassion and true caring. Having the option of ending a terminally ill person's life early—along with the possibly implicit coercion to do so—will not improve the quality of care given to such patients and may in fact lead to even worse care for those who do *not* choose euthanasia. The problems health care professionals have in dealing with dying patients are well documented. How will they feel when the patient could have "already checked out" but has chosen not to? Similarly, it troubles me that a society that does such a poor job of providing a minimum of decent health care for many of its members, and often offers only impersonal, non-compassionate care for those who receive any at all, can be seriously considering making available a vehicle for eliminating many of the people who most need genuine care and treatment.

Perhaps in rare and extreme cases, as I suggested at the beginning of this statement, faced with no good choice, the Christian must follow Martin Luther's advice and "sin boldly," knowing that divine grace is sufficient for forgiveness of an act even so contrary to God's will. With this caveat, however, my answer to the question posed is that, as a matter of principle and policy, active euthanasia, even if voluntary and restricted to clear expressions of desire on the part of the patient, is best not practiced.

6

SHOULD WE HAVE A PUBLIC POLICY?

In discussions of active voluntary euthanasia, the issue of the morality of euthanasia in the individual case frequently is conflated with the issue of the morality of a public policy that legalizes euthanasia. Many would argue that they are distinct though related issues. The first is a matter of individual morality, while the second is one of social morality. Many people might believe that euthanasia was justified in one or more of the cases presented in Chapter 1. But it doesn't follow from such a judgment that euthanasia should be permitted on a societal scale. Conversely, a public policy permitting active voluntary euthanasia does not necessarily settle the moral justifiability of euthanasia in individual cases. Different considerations and criteria come into play when we move from an individual to a societal context and vice versa.

In what follows, we strive to give the matter of public policy its own hearing. Contributors to this section were asked to respond to this question: "Would it be desirable to develop a public policy that would permit physicians (or other specially designated agents) directly to end the lives of terminally ill patients who are not able to carry out assisted suicide and who request to have their lives ended?" Again, the perspectives are varied, and although these reflections may not be comprehensive, we hope they will provoke further reflection and discussion.

REFLECTION

Margaret Murphy, Ph.D., R.N.

I believe it would be desirable to develop a public policy to permit active voluntary euthanasia of terminally ill patients who are not able to carry out assisted suicide and who request to have their lives ended. However, I believe that this policy should be allowed only in certain delimited circumstances: (1) when the patient has clearly made this request repeatedly and without coercion; and (2) when the patient has an incurable, painful illness that is terminal *or* has impending or actual permanent loss of mental capacity.

In addition, I think the policy would need to include a review process involving health care professionals, ethicists, and the patient or his or her designated surrogate to assure that the conditions noted above had been met and to avoid precipitate action or abuse.

I take this position after much reflection and deliberation. As a nurse who has concentrated most of her career on working with older adults, I have seen and heard many of the dilemmas associated with this issue. I do not take it lightly, nor do I make *age* a condition. I do not believe that age, by itself, is a criterion for any decision related to death. Rather, I make the following assumptions:

1. Death is not an absolute evil to be avoided at all costs and in all circumstances, and life is not an absolute good to be preserved and maintained at all costs.

2. Human life is more than biological functioning. It includes self-awareness and the ability to reason, emote, communicate, decide, and attach meaning—at least at some level.

3. Keeping a human being alive against his or her own will after all dignity, appreciation, and meaning of life have ceased and any benefit to anyone is impossible is cruel and dehumanizing.

4. Individuals have the right to a dignified and gentle death when faced with incurable and painful illness.

I would intentionally not restrict the policy to circumstances in which death was *imminent,* to allow for the inclusion of persons with intractable, ultimately terminal, illness affecting mental or brain function such as Alzheimer's disease. Such illnesses can destroy those capabilities that make life worth living long before they result in biological death. Without a policy that allows the option of active voluntary euthanasia for those persons who believe life to be over when cognitive function ceases, two choices remain: (1) to request that direct, voluntary euthanasia be performed while they retain many cognitive abilities; or (2) to continue to function biologically and in a personally degrading manner long after their cognitive abilities have ceased. It seems to me that each is a travesty.

Some will say that developing a public policy for active voluntary euthanasia puts us on the "slippery slope" to involuntary euthanasia. This need not be true, however, where citizens have the right to design *and* repeal public policy that is noxious to them. In addition, given a carefully constructed policy with specific circumstantial guidelines, there is no reason to believe that these would be easily expanded in our society. The policy under consideration is *VOLUNTARY,* that is, the person must have requested it and have done so repeatedly. In my view, there exists today far more abuse on the opposite end of the spectrum—painful, undignified deaths extended by the "miracles of technology."

My greatest fear is that if such a policy were actually drafted, it would be so hedged by rules and regulations as to make it useless. This has been the case with much living will legislation and litigation. The challenge is to draw up a policy broad enough to include and protect the wishes of all who wish to use it, without leaving it too open to abuse or challenges by others. This is a formidable challenge, and, unfortunately, one that we as a society are probably not yet ready to undertake. Before such a policy can be successfully adopted, much discussion and education need to take place. All positions need to be publicly aired and carefully considered so that the electorate can affect policy development and implementation. Thus, although I favor a policy that permits active voluntary euthanasia under certain circumstances, I do not hold much hope for its adoption in the near future.

REFLECTION

Robert Moss, M.D.

During the past 25 years, significant advances in medicine have enabled physicians to extend life beyond limits previously thought possible. For many the introduction of these newer technologies offers the hope of a prolonged and productive life, while for the less fortunate they appear to do nothing more than prolong the process of dying and human suffering. In our attempts to add quality years to our lives, the distinction between what is living and what is dying has become more artificial. We have redefined what it means to die by turning it into an unnatural process, often obtainable through the withdrawal of life-supporting therapies. And it is partially because of this transformation of death that we have been forced to look at ourselves, challenge our own ethics, and redefine our moral priorities.

The past decade in medical ethics and case law has been dominated, in a way, by our attempts to recapture the essence and meaning of this so-called good death. Policies on the withholding and withdrawal of life-sustaining therapies have afforded some individuals the opportunity to "die with dignity," but for an increasingly demanding public these policies have not gone far enough. During the past two years, active voluntary euthanasia, or the purposeful termination of a patient's life to prevent further suffering, has been debated in both the lay press and medical literature. The debate has been intensified by such articles as "It's Over, Debbie" published in the *Journal of the American Medical Association* and more recently the story of Dr. Kevorkian and his "suicide machine" published in newspapers across the country. Further, both public opinion polls and physician surveys have demonstrated increasing support for euthanasia. An unsuccessful attempt was recently made in California to pass by referendum the Humane and Dignified Death Act, which would have legalized euthanasia. Such efforts to legalize euthanasia will be made again this year in Washington, Florida, and Oregon.

Yet there are strong societal, religious, and legal prohibitions against taking the life of another individual, and euthanasia therefore remains punishable under general criminal statutes in all 50 states. Leading ethicists and physicians have made forceful arguments against any public policy supporting the legalization of euthanasia. That doctors must not violate this 2,500-year-old proscription given in the Hippocratic oath is also the position of the Council on Ethical and Judicial Affairs of the American Medical Association. "I will give no deadly drug to any, though it be asked of me, nor will I counsel such." To hasten death in this manner challenges the essence of the physician's identity as healer and would begin to erode the faith and trust that patients have in their doctors.

Some have also expressed grave concerns that active euthanasia would be a dangerous precedent for public policy because of its potential for indiscriminate use against vulnerable groups. Examples of such abuse have been reported in the Netherlands, where euthanasia remains illegal but is generally tolerated and supported by case law. Further, the growing pressures to contain costs may have an adverse impact on such a public policy: less trustworthy individuals may ultimately consider euthanasia a cost-effective way to treat chronic illness. Practical problems like defining the terms associated with euthanasia—*suffering, terminal illness, and competency*"can make such a policy difficult to implement. Insuring voluntariness and

125

protecting vulnerable groups of people are additional concerns when safeguards have not been tested.

Proponents argue that euthanasia is both morally and legally acceptable. They see no moral distinction between the withdrawal and withholding of life-sustaining therapies and active voluntary euthanasia where the motives or intent, human responses and results are often the same. Such boundaries between passive and active euthanasia become almost indistinguishable when one is considering withdrawing a patient from a ventilator or administering morphine to alleviate not pain but respiratory distress. It is argued further that through the principle of autonomy, competent patients possess the right to have their death mercifully hastened when they are terminally ill and are suffering from intolerable pain. The preservation of life in these instances may be an inappropriate goal, and the honoring of such wishes may be viewed positively as enhancing autonomy and respect for persons.

Several important issues need further attention on both sides of the debate. Does the desire for euthanasia signify the failure of the medical profession to consider the comfort goals and needs of our hopelessly ill patients? If so, can these needs be better met through alternative ways of controlling pain and providing comfort? Even if euthanasia is morally acceptable, is it appropriate to legalize it and therefore make it possibly obligatory? Would a more conservative law afford greater protection for our vulnerable populations?

For the physician, euthanasia is a moral dilemma created by conflicting duties: the duty to do no harm and the duty to alleviate suffering. Although some authorities have ranked these duties, it is still difficult to know whether one harms a patient more by hastening his death and alleviating his suffering or by not hastening his death and allowing his suffering to continue. With a patient one has known for a long time, deciding which is the more caring and compassionate act is often not difficult to do.

I believe that active voluntary euthanasia is morally justified in exceptional circumstances. Such circumstances can be determined by applying many of the guidelines developed by the Dutch Medical Society. The request for euthanasia should be voluntary and made by a competent patient who has a terminal illness and is suffering from intractable pain. Such a request should be made repeatedly and consistently. All possible treatment modalities should be offered first to try to control pain and keep the patient comfortable. If these efforts fail, euthanasia can be considered, preferably by the patient's personal physician and within the context of a long-standing trusting relationship. An opinion from a second physician or designated review committee should be obtained to enhance objectivity and diffuse responsibility. Euthanasia should not be obligatory for physicians who are morally opposed to this procedure. Full disclosure of the process should take place after euthanasia is performed.

It is clear that active voluntary euthanasia takes us to the limits of both patient and physician autonomy and must be approached with great caution and respect. We cannot, however, ignore our responsibility to address growing public sentiment and the unmet needs of suffering patients who are the victims of our own interventions. To do so could further erode the trust that patients have in their doctors and even promote the proliferation of less scrupulous physicians who would be willing to perform euthanasia more indiscriminately. As physicians, we must make greater efforts to comfort and alleviate the pain and suffering of dying patients and insure that they are not abandoned. Only under exceptional circumstances, when the needs of our patients cannot be met otherwise, and in accordance with the guidelines above, should active voluntary euthanasia be considered an alternative from a public policy perspective.

REFLECTION

Don C. Shaw

Until about 50 years ago most deaths occurred in the home. Death was a reality that people knew they would have to deal with sooner or later. Doctors visited seriously ill patients in their homes and at some point would usually inform the family that death was inevitable and that there was nothing more they could do other than prescribe a few medications to control some of the pain. Family and friends would then watch over the dying person and give whatever loving care they could until the end came.

Since that time the rapid development of new medical and surgical techniques has conquered many diseases and restored health to millions of men, women, and children. I myself would probably have died in 1963 were it not for the development of penicillin only a few years earlier.

But there was also a very dark side to these vast new developments. Increasingly life was being extended even when hope of recovery had long since gone. Life for many was reduced to "biological existence" with no quality of life and the dying process prolonged for months and even years. As of this writing more than 10,000 American adults remain in nursing homes and hospitals in vegetative comas with no hope of recovery at the horrendous public expense of $350,000,000 each year. They're kept alive largely because there is no documented evidence that they would have chosen to be allowed to die.

In view of these medical advancements, passive euthanasia (allowing the withdrawal of respirators, feeding tubes, and other medical and surgical techniques from the terminally ill and those in a vegetative coma) became an issue of major debate during the 1970s and the 1980s. Judicial and legislative decisions increasingly supported the right to passive euthanasia if it was the patient's personal choice and if the choice had been made when the patient was competent.

In the 1980s the concept of voluntary active euthanasia began to gain public attention, largely due to the work of the National Hemlock Society, founded in 1980. Obviously active euthanasia could best be handled by doctors, thus the phrase "physician aid in dying."

Physician aid in dying is indeed desirable and urgently needed but only when given at the voluntary request of the patient and only if the patient is terminally ill. At present, Holland is the only nation in the world where active euthanasia is being practiced by physicians. It has not been legalized by the Dutch Parliament but rather by a long series of judicial decisions that began in the mid-1970s.

In April 1990 a poll was taken by the Roper Organization of a cross-section of 1,978 American men and women, 18 or over, interviewed in face-to-face interviews in the respondents' homes. The leading question asked was, "When a person has a painful and distressing terminal disease, do you think doctors should or should not be allowed by law to end the patient's life if there is no hope of recovery and the patient requests it?" The poll results: Yes, 64 percent (1,264); No, 24 percent (465); Don't know, 13 percent (248). Such findings are confirmed by numerous other polls and studies done throughout the U. S. There is no doubt that the majority of Americans favor physician aid in dying when voluntarily requested by the terminally ill.

There is also a general consensus among legal and medical experts regarding the rules that should govern physician aid in dying. In ordinary language the rules are these:

1. The patient's physician must affirm that in his or her judgment the patient indeed is terminally ill and there is no hope of recovery. If the physician is unwilling to perform euthanasia, another must be found who is willing.

2. A second physician must confirm the diagnosis and prognosis of the first physician.

3. The terminally ill patient must have requested physician aid in dying while competent and repeated his or her request on several occasions and in the presence of two or more witnesses.

4. Noncompetent terminally ill patients may be given physician aid in dying if they had prepared a legal document prior to their terminal condition requesting such aid in dying in the event that they became terminally ill.

5. Adult citizens may execute a legal document in which they appoint an agent or guardian to make all medical decisions, including aid in dying, on their behalf if and when they become terminally ill and are not competent to make such decisions for themselves.

In the recent U.S. Supreme Court decision regarding Nancy Cruzan and the Missouri Supreme Court, the Court ruled that the Missouri Supreme Court was correct in requiring that Nancy Cruzan be kept alive by artificial nutrition and hydration in view of the fact that she had never documented her wishes for passive euthanasia in the event of a terminal illness or a comatose vegetative condition. This decision stimulated a public response of a magnitude rarely seen. Hundreds of thousands of ordinary American citizens—mostly middle-aged and elderly but also a surprising number of younger adults—have for the first time ever obtained and executed living wills and power of attorney for health care documents. Under present laws these documents give people the legal right to passive euthanasia in the event of terminal illness or a comatose vegetative condition.

In view of the 1990 Roper poll (taken several months before the Supreme Court's *Cruzan* decision), it is abundantly clear that American citizens will in the near future obtain the legal right to physician aid in dying. As of this writing a vigorous campaign is under way in the state of Washington to legalize physician aid in dying in 1991 [Initiative 119, discussed by Albert R. Jonsen, below]. Once such legislation is enacted in one state, others are sure to follow. Ralph Mero, president of the Hemlock Society of Washington State and prime activist in the campaign there, has stated the issue clearly:

> Death with dignity simply means the opportunity to choose a death without pain, without fear, and without physical, mental or spiritual degradation. It is the right to retain

control of the final stage of one's existence, and to affirm even to the last one's self-respect. Such a choice must be without coercion, freely chosen out of one's own integrity as consistent with a dignified life. Now is the time to let a dying person determine the final step of one's own life journey, and be allowed to say goodbye before the process of dying has stolen away the quality of life, leaving behind only the empty shell of what was once a beautiful human being.

Obviously, there are those who oppose both passive and active euthanasia and for a variety of reasons. Some are opposed on philosophical and religious grounds. Their beliefs are fully respected by the proponents of euthanasia. They are most often Roman Catholic and fundamentalist Christians. Other opponents contend that legalizing euthanasia will open the door to abuse and lead to the killing of the handicapped, the elderly, and others who are a burden to society. Our response to this latter group is that every good known to humankind can be abused. It is our responsibility as a civilized society to see to it that such abuses are not permitted.

REFLECTION

Albert R. Jonsen

(The following was originally written as a letter to the Washington State Medical Association in response to Initiative 119, which sought the legalization of active euthanasia. It provides a response to an actual public policy proposal.)

First, it must be acknowledged that the principal issue, namely, the appropriate care of the terminally ill person, deserves serious attention. It seems obvious that the interest in Initiative 119 comes from the concerns of people that they will not be treated appropriately when the time comes. Many horror stories are heard when the Initiative is discussed; unfortunately, many of them are true, and many are the result of the ignorance and insensitivity of some physicians about appropriate care of the dying patient. Many of them also result from the crude state of the law, and the even cruder state of its understanding by the public, physicians, and lawyers. Thus the entire issue of appropriate care for the terminally ill deserves discussion and clarification. The sponsors of Initiative 119 are to be thanked for pushing this question to the fore. The medical profession should, on its part, respond in a positive way.

The popular discussion of the Initiative reveals that the broad concern about appropriate care is at the root of the matter. It is, for example, very common to find that discussants mix up the question of forgoing life support, which is clearly ethical in the appropriate circumstances and is supported by the medical profession and the law, with the question of active euthanasia. They seem to argue that "doctors and the law will not let people die; therefore we should permit doctors legally to 'assist in dying,' i.e., commit active euthanasia." This is, of course, a gross logical fallacy, as well as a mistaken impression about what medicine and the law actually do.

It is important to note that Initiative 119 takes up three topics, two of which the profession can, with some reservations, support. First, it proposes that persistent vegetative state should be considered a *terminal* condition. This is, I think, a mistaken route to a correct goal. PVS is not technically a terminal condition, since the pathology itself is not lethal; it can be *made* terminal by forgoing medically mediated nutrition and hydration. Many ethicists, with concurrence by the President's Commission for the Study of Ethical Problems in Medicine, agree that life-sustaining measures, including nutrition and hydration, can be omitted for patients in PVS. Thus it is not necessary to take the semantic route of changing the designation to terminal, except that the relevant legislation, Washington's Natural Death Act, defines terminal so narrowly.

Second, the Initiative proposes that artificial nutrition and hydration should be defined as life-sustaining measures that can be removed at the request of patient or family. This corresponds to the position of ethicists and of most medical organizations, such as the American Medical Association and the American College of Physicians. It is a wise provision in view of the *Cruzan* decision.

The third topic, "aid in dying," poses much more difficult ethical problems. In my opinion, it is not compatible with the ethics of medicine and should not be supported by the organized profession.

Aid in dying poses a significant challenge to contemporary physicians. The challenge is not entirely new: physicians have always faced the agonized patient who pleaded for relief of pain even if it meant the release of death. The words, "I will give no deadly poison to any patient even if asked," would certainly not have been inserted in the Hippocratic oath unless ancient physicians had been asked. Many physicians, ancient and modern, have quietly and secretly acceded to that request and have felt they were right to have done so. Others have struggled with their consciences and refused. These are not new problems in medicine.

The new challenge is the proposal that physicians be immunized from the law when they respond to a request for aid in dying. They and they alone would be legally delegated to enter into a compact with a patient to perform actions designed to end the patient's life. This would reintroduce into our moral culture a practice that was slowly and painfully abolished centuries ago: the practice of private killing.

By drawing killing out of the realm of private transactions, such as the personal vendetta and the private revenge, into the harsh light of law, society attempts to restrain the inevitable tendency for abuse by forcing anyone who kills to defend the action publicly. The ancient commentators on revenge often saw little wrong in revenge itself: it was frequently seen as justified. Rather they were concerned that the anger inherent in revenge would carry the justifiable practice much further to the great detriment of a peaceful society. So today, even when a particular act of euthanasia might be morally justifiable (and hypothetically one might be), the force of the compassion that motivates it might also drive our acceptance of the practice of killing those in pain and distress beyond the careful limits we may set around it (and which Initiative 119 does set). In my view, the reintroduction of private killing is a step backward in our struggle to build a moral culture.

It is not enough to assert that, unlike the anger and vengeance that motivated the vendetta, this new form of private killing rests on an inherently moral motive, compassion. Compassion is indeed a moral motive, but it is not in itself a justification for all behavior. Compassion for the poor may inspire Robin Hoods, and yet society must repudiate private redistributions of property. Compassion for the oppressed may inspire terrorism, yet even those who espouse the cause of the oppressed may find terrorism an unacceptable instrument of liberation. It has been, and in some places, still is, thought to be an act of compassion to put a heretic or blasphemer out of the misery of their ignorance. Compassion, then, while noble, is not itself sufficient to render an action morally acceptable.

Similarly, it is not enough to assert that the voluntary request of the recipient of aid in dying renders it morally acceptable. We do place high value on the autonomy of persons as the grounds of morality. Yet we should be reluctant to accept autonomy as the sole determinant of morality. Persons can freely choose life-styles and actions that we might, on other grounds, consider immoral, even when they do not directly cause harm to others. For example, it is difficult totally to absolve from immorality someone who abuses his or her mind and body to the point of destruction; the thoroughly selfish and self-indulgent person is hardly deserving of praise, even when his or her actions do not directly harm someone else. Thus, the voluntary nature of aid in dying is not sufficient to give it moral status.

The moral status of any action depends on a whole complex of features. Motives, circumstances, immediate and remote consequences, its exemplary effects on persons and institutions—all these are relevant to a judgment of morality. Thus we are accustomed to saying, "On the whole, I think this or that is right or wrong." As can be seen from this letter, "on the whole," I think that Initiative 119 is wrong, as is the practice of voluntary euthanasia which it sanctions.

Some might object that physicians are already involved in private killing: their patients die as the result of physicians' decisions to forgo further treatment, particularly life-sustaining treatments. Is there any real difference, they say, between dying as the result of turning off a respirator and dying as the result of a lethal injection? If one isn't properly called "killing" and isn't legally actionable, why should the other be? There are complex philosophical answers to these questions, involving "permitting" and "committing," "acting" and "omitting," and so on, but even philosophers find them too complicated and often misleading and illogical. The one real meaning that attaches to all these distinctions is that in the case of death caused by a physician's decision that further treatment is futile or unlikely to restore health, the physician stops doing what he or she no longer has any duty to do. The patient's death then comes about because there is no longer anything "helpful" that medicine can offer.

This becomes clear when we notice that Initiative 119 would identify "aid in dying" as a "new medical procedure." This is a strange designation for several reasons. First, the exact nature of the procedure is not specified: it is a procedure without any of the usual features of a medical procedure, that is, indications, instruments, maneuvers, dosages, standards of practice, and so on. We are left to wonder what it is. If it is *any sort* of action that will cause death, then there is no reason to call it a "medical procedure." One can cause death with suffocation, an electric wire, a club, a gun, a poison. Relatively little medical skill is required to use any of these. If it is supposed that a quick, clean death requires a physician's competence in choosing and using drugs, it *might* be described as a medical procedure (although many physicians would probably bungle the job without special training). But then its rank as a medical procedure comes under suspicion for another reason: medical procedures are ethically required to promote the benefit of the patient, and traditionally that benefit has been interpreted as improving a patient's health. This is a new medical procedure indeed because it, and it alone, does not have this goal. Among all the medical procedures that make up medical practice, aid in dying achieves a unique goal, the termination of the patient's life. This might be defined by the patient as a benefit, but it certainly cannot be construed as improving the patient's health.

This new medical procedure does, however, have some peculiar implications. If it is considered something doctors can perform, it should be made known to patients whether the doctor *will* perform it. This must become an element in any adequate informed consent. Physicians are ethically and legally required to present to a patient all options open to the patient. If aid in dying is accepted as a "new medical procedure," it then constitutes an option open to the patient. Doctors, then, will have the duty to inform patients of this option at the beginning of their relationship and will need to indicate their willingness or reluctance to carry out aid in dying.

This itself may affect the therapeutic relationship in peculiar ways. After a diagnosis of some serious but still treatable disease, a patient should be informed not merely of the option of no treatment but also of the option of aid in dying. A patient may choose no treatment, together with aid in dying at the point that the disease can be designated, by two physicians, as "terminal." In that case, the physician will have never served as a therapist, but only as an assistant in dying. Alternatively, the patient may choose to accept treatment (say chemotherapy) while retaining the right to switch to aid in dying at any point in the course. This switch may take place at some particularly low point in the course of the therapy where discouragement may dominate the decision. The whole course of therapy will be conducted with this possibility hanging over it. Physicians should reflect whether this new medical procedure may introduce significant changes in their relationships with their patients.

Initiative 119 clearly attempts to restrict the ambiguities that might make the introduction of this new medical procedure suspect and unpalatable. Thus it is limited to those patients who have been declared "terminally" ill by two physicians. This, however, introduces more ambiguities than it eliminates. Does this mean terminally ill in the sense of having a diagnosis usually associated with death regardless of treatment, a diagnosis associated with low probabilities of survival with treatment, or a diagnosis that has a good prognosis with treatment but inevitable death without it? This is not clear, yet it is important for the legal parameters of the practice of aid in dying.

In addition, the term *terminally ill* usually has been applied to none of the above. The term usually designates a condition in which death is imminent regardless of treatment. If this is the sense to be used in application of aid in dying, it is possible that physicians will hesitate to make this designation until all therapeutic possibilities have been exhausted. Thus some persons who seek assistance in death will be put through the entire course of treatment before it can be provided. Presumably, this is what many of them would wish to avoid. Also, many might wish to avoid the prospect of a long, demeaning deterioration, as is seen in the tragic course of Alzheimer's patients. People facing this prospect may wish to escape it, but aid in dying will not be available to them because they cannot be said to be terminally ill. Thus even the compassionate motives and the voluntary nature of proposed aid in dying will often be frustrated.

It is clear that Initiative 119 wishes to reserve this new medical procedure for the voluntary, competent patients. It is less clear that, once established, patients will be free of coercion to request it. The coercion may be subtle and unspoken, but families distressed by their relative's illness may hint at it as a way out. Patients may themselves feel that they are undue burdens on their families and so should remove themselves. It is a voluntary option that has coercive possibilities. The same may be true for the physician. While Initiative 119 does not require a physician to participate in aid in dying, it is possible that many reluctant physicians will come under pressure from patients and families to do so. It would be particularly tragic for a physician who has moral scruples about aid in dying to find himself or herself petitioned by a long-time, devoted patient and forced to refuse this last request.

It seems to me that the two considerations above make up the "slippery slope" that we worry about with proposals like Initiative 119. In itself, it attempts to make legal a very limited, carefully restricted activity. However, the limited activity is so limited that it fails to meet the needs of the people who support it. If they want relief from deterioration and future pain, 119 cannot give them that—it can only provide relief after these have come. Thus, there may be pressure to make the legalized action more liberal, allowing people to choose aid in dying before deterioration and pain appear. This is a first slip down the slope. Initiative 119 applies only to the competent, voluntary patient, but much of the pain and distress of dying comes to the incompetent and to their families. 119 cannot help them. Thus there may be an inclination to extend the scope of the legalized action to those who "would certainly have wished it, had they been able." Of course, these pressures and inclinations cannot be certainly predicted, and perhaps, if they do appear, can be resisted, but the "slippery slope" argument suggests that, given the nature of the problem, they are not improbable and that they will be difficult to resist.

Finally, one of the noblest of the ancient duties of physicians is to relieve pain. Hippocrates wrote that it is the physician's work "to assuage pain, to lessen the violence of disease, and to refrain from treating those whom the disease has overcome." Relief of pain has become a fine art in recent years. Many procedures and techniques, from the surgical to the psychological, have been added to the medical armamentarium. Indeed, traditional medical ethics allowed physicians to relieve the pain of dying even at risk of causing death. The permission to effect death directly by lethal administration goes beyond this. It transforms a risk into a certainty. It relieves the patient's pain by eliminating the patient. However, another possible consequence flows from this permission: it may attenuate the impetus toward more effective modes of pain relief. If pain can be ended by the death of the patient, why persist in the careful titration of medicine and emotional support that relieves pain and, at the same time, supports life?

These, then, are some of the considerations that lead me to conclude that the social and legal acceptance of aid in dying would be most unfortunate for physicians and for the profession. I consider this new medical practice to be unethical for all these reasons. My judgment does not in itself rest on the distinctions between direct and indirect, active and passive, and so on, that philosophers fight over (although I do find some meaning in them). I am in full agreement with the position stated in the Ethics Manual of the American College of Physicians: "even if legalized, euthanasia should be considered contrary to the ethics of medicine."

Some have raised an issue that deserves some comment. They note that the ethics of medicine no longer prohibits abortion (although an individual physician's ethics may). They wonder how it is possible to allow killing of the fetus and to prohibit killing of the dying. Much can be said about this question, but here it suffices to note only two points. First, the distinction is morally acceptable on the grounds that the fetus does not have the status of a human person. This is a plausible position; its opposite can also be plausibly maintained. Clearly, however, neither position is established. On this ground, the permissibility of abortion can be distinguished from the impermissibility of euthanasia. A second reason can be offered, namely, that ethical abortion, as distinguished from legal abortion, requires that the continuation of the pregnancy be a threat to maternal life. In such cases, the ethics of abortion are equivalent to the ethics of self-defense. Admittedly, in the era of abortion by choice this argument appears old-fashioned. Still, I believe many physicians prefer to see abortion as ethical only on the basis of some sort of medical indications. To the extent that this is so, it is possible to distinguish between abortion and euthanasia.

REFLECTION

Albert W. Alschuler

We dread these decisions. When should we allow death to come even though we might, through ordinary or extraordinary action, preserve life? When, if ever, should we act affirmatively to bring life to an end? Rather than confront these issues, we may conclude that we should do what we can to preserve life and then leave it to fate or to God to decide.

This view might have been plausible when our medical efforts *in extremis* were gallant, quick, and unsuccessful—in particular, when we were unable to maintain "vegetative" pateints for extended periods. Almost no one takes this view today. All of us seem agreed that we need not—and should not—take extraordinary measures to preserve life in all circumstances. Justice Scalia spoke in this year's *Cruzan* decision of "the constantly increasing power of science to keep the human body alive for longer than any reasonable person would want to inhabit it," and our best judgment is that a majority of the two million deaths that occur each year in the U.S. now follow a decision to forgo some life-sustaining treatment. "A time to be born, and a time to die." There comes a time to let go of life, to *choose* to let it pass.

This recognition of responsibility brings a rush of other decisions. To invoke the familiar metaphor, we find ourselves on a slippery slope. Once we have decided to let go of life, what sorts of support and treatment may we appropriately discontinue?

Twenty years ago, few physicians believed that the withdrawal of an unconscious patient's nutrition or hydration was ever appropriate. Today four dissenting Justices of the Supreme Court believe that the withdrawal of nutrition is a constitutional right, one that in some circumstances may be exercised on behalf of an unconscious patient by others.

The reasons suggested for distinguishing the withdrawal of a feeding tube from the withdrawal of other forms of treatment may seem strained; and once we allow the withdrawal of nutrition and hydration, it becomes almost equally difficult to maintain the next line. The next line, moreover, is the one upon which we have insisted most vigorously—the line between permitting a person to die, on the one hand, and killing or aiding suicide, on the other.

What is to be said in favor of a patient's slow, certain death by starvation when an injection could bring the same result more quickly and perhaps with less pain? What is to be said in favor of preserving the old line between feasance and nonfeasance, action and inaction?

This line has been central to our law of homicide, just as it has been central to interpretations of the biblical commandment not to kill. A sadist who laughs rather than reach down to save a child from falling into a fire is guilty of no crime. A wife who, after deliberation, uses poison to end the suffering of a beloved, terminally ill, incompetent husband commits first-degree murder.

In the twentieth century, we must more and more judge behavior by its consequences. To a consequentialist, the line between feasance and nonfeasance is likely to seem silly. Why fuss about metaphysics when the outcome will not be affected? We have made the largest decision—to let life end. Why resist the quickest and least agonizing method of bringing this result about?

Many of us, fortunately, have twelfth-century rather than twentieth-century minds. We are not bottom-line consequentialists. We do sense a difference between causing death and failing to prevent it. The line between feasance and nonfeasance, however, may mark only roughly the moral boundary that we seek.

A California case illustrates the artificiality of this line. With the concurrence of the family of a patient in a vegetative state which the court said was "likely" to be permanent, two physicians disconnected the patient's respirator. The patient continued to breathe; and several days later, again with the family's approval, the physicians withdrew the intravenous tubes providing his nutrition and hydration. Following the patient's death, a prosecutor charged the physicians with murder, and a trial court refused to dismiss the charges against them. On appeal, another court characterized the physicians' behavior as an omission—a failure to provide affirmative assistance to the patient. This court ordered the murder charges dismissed.

One wonders whether the California appellate court would have viewed the case in the same way if an enemy of the patient had entered his hospital room and disconnected the respirator and intravenous tubes. Our impulse in this situation surely would be to treat "pulling the plug" as an affirmative act. Of course there are differences between the two cases, but they are not captured by the act-omission line. Physically, the behavior in both cases was the same.

The morally relevant line is not between physical action and inaction. It is between failing to improve the "normal" human condition and worsening this normal condition. In a laissez-faire world in which the norm is inaction—in which people usually leave one another alone—the physical line often may appear plausible. But we have increasingly left this world behind.

Homicide law itself recognizes that the appropriate standard is not always a physical line. This law identifies a number of special relationships in which the "normal" condition is one of care, and it imposes a duty to provide the care expected in these relationships. A parent's failure to care for a child, for example, worsens the child's normal condition. If the parent's omission causes death, the parent bears the same criminal responsibility as if he had caused the child's death through an affirmative act. (Because a physician has a contractual duty to care for her patients, the physician's failure to provide care similarly can lead to criminal responsibility. In the California case, however, the court concluded that the physicians had satisfied their contractual duty to provide reasonable care. If the court had characterized the defendants' withdrawal of life support as an act, no "defense" of reasonableness would have been available, and the defendants apparently would have been guilty of murder.) Apart from "special relationship" cases, homicide law treats the social norm as inaction. It draws the physical line between feasance and nonfeasance.

Although this line is troublesome, no other baseline, either normative or sociological, is apparent. We have no clear picture of "normal" human entitlements in a world in which feeding tubes can maintain one's life in a persistent vegetative state for 30 years or more.

We may easily conclude that an enemy's interruption of approved medical treatment diminishes the "normal" human condition, but we are less confident of the baseline for judging the physicians' behavior. Is the normal condition of someone in a persistent vegetative state starvation because this person cannot feed herself? Or is the provision of nutrition, even through an intravenous tube, part of the baseline entitlement of human beings? Our practices change rapidly. Our standards seem up for grabs.

In this situation, the strongest argument for the action-inaction line is that, despite its indeterminacy and imprecision, we need it. We have no other line, and without it we sense no limits. Shall we impose an affirmative obligation to reach out to save a drowning child? What, then, of the mother who refuses to approve the donation of some of her child's bone marrow to save the life of the child's half-brother? What of the physician who refuses to fly to Calcutta (or to walk across the hall) to perform a lifesaving operation that she alone can perform? What of the person who purchases a stereo rather than send $1,000 to the famine relief fund?

Even as we recognize the artificiality of the action-inaction line, we hesitate to impose new affirmative duties. Similarly, we hesitate to authorize traditionally prohibited acts that, we realize, cannot be neatly distinguished from permissible omissions. We may forbid assisted suicide and active euthanasia while recognizing that the alternative is likely to be the withdrawal of medication or nutrition—and a death that may be equally chosen but that will be accompanied by greater suffering. We have no very strong conviction that the line to which we cling is the correct one; but once we cross this line, where will we stop? Where does the slippery slope hit bottom?

Perhaps assisted suicide or active euthanasia is appropriate for a cancer patient facing only a few more weeks or months of agony before death. If so, is it also appropriate for someone like Janet Adkins? Adkins was the woman who, following a diagnosis of Alzheimer's disease, used Dr. Kevorkian's suicide machine to end her life in the back of a rusty Volkswagen van. She did so a week after she had beaten her 33-year-old son at tennis and had enjoyed a last romantic weekend with her husband.

What appear to be individual and private decisions may shape our culture. Adkins had begun at 54 to lose her memory; she could no longer play the music that she loved; she presumably hoped that her friends and family would remember her as a vibrant person; she did not wish to become a burden, draining other lives along with her own. Our stewardship of earthly resources includes stewardship of the most precious earthly resource of all, our lives. Did Adkins make an appropriate stewardship decision?

If so, what about Gramps? His memory is largely gone; he can no longer control his bladder; he isn't nearly as much fun as he once was. The death of Gramps would sadden us of course, but wouldn't it be for the best if he showed the same consideration for friends and family and made the same responsible decision that Janet Adkins did? As we move the line of what is permissible, we may move the line of what is expected. Gramps may seek the counsel of his offspring, and they may answer that they cannot advise him. Gramps must make the decision for himself. As attorney Yale Kamisar has suggested, consensual euthanasia could "sweep up some who are not really tired of life but think others are tired of them." Subtle pressures may encourage the newly acceptable choice.

Or more than subtle pressures. When a person's living will says "don't touch the plug," her insurance company may charge a higher premium. This person's desire to prolong her life may cost the company money. Someone whose living will says "pull the plug early," however, may receive a discount.

I need not go step-by-step down the slippery slope. Its lowest point has been described by science fiction writers. In an uncaring world (which I do not suggest is just around the corner), we might be encouraged, expected, or even required to visit Dr. Kevorkian's van as soon as we could no longer be productive.

For myself, I would, with trepidation, abandon the action-inaction line to permit a person to consent to active euthanasia in a case of severe pain resulting from an incurable, fatal illness or in a case of irreversible coma. I would require an unambiguous authorization given during the current disability or earlier—perhaps in a living will. I would permit euthanasia, however, only after a judicial hearing at which a guardian would be assigned to argue against it and at which a judge would consider the patient's competency, the clarity and voluntariness of her choice, and the possibility of her recovery from the illness, coma, or disability. A judicial inquiry, with the brief delay that it would entail, would help insure that a recent choice was the product of serious reflection rather than short-term discouragement or depression. (Despite my twelfth-century mind, I can be moved a little by consequentialist arguments.)

This first step across the historic divide might not in fact go far enough, but it seems best to proceed slowly—and it is easier to move further down the slope than to climb back up. In particular, I would not permit any sort of substituted judgment for comatose or otherwise incompetent patients who had not voiced their desires. For some patients, then, the incongruity of authorizing the slower death and not the quicker, the omission and not the act, would remain; but I would not authorize affirmative action to kill a human being without that person's consent—a consent that could not be hypothesized.

In some wrenching situations, I confess that I might be less hesitant about euthanasia than I have suggested the legislature should be. As a boy, I once hastened the death of a possum that had been badly mauled by a dog. Because no more appropriate killing instrument was at hand, I used a rock to crush the creature's skull. I recall the occasion with horror, but I believe that my action was right and that failing to act would not have been. I do not know why an appropriate act of mercy for a possum would not also be one for a human being in equally hopeless circumstances.

As these strange musings suggest, the issues are imponderable. In a sense, it is every person for herself. In an equally significant sense, however, it is all of us together. We must struggle as a community to resolve these issues, recognizing that our own answers are fallible and that others' are worthy of respect. In *Cruzan*, the Supreme Court wisely declined to take these issues from us.

I doubt that Providence works in quite this way, but it is almost as though God had led us to face these issues. God once permitted us to believe that none of these decisions were ours to make. It is much more difficult to take that view today.

English legal history offers something of a parallel. Eight hundred years ago, people believed that judging criminal guilt was too terrifying a task to entrust to mere mortals. These people sought the judgment of God through forms of trial like the ordeal, which left the outcome largely to fate or chance. In 1215, the Fourth Lateran Council under Pope Innocent III forbade the ordeal; and for a century thereafter, our English forebears struggled uncomfortably toward an alternative. They eventually settled on trial by jury, a somewhat less mystical institution. As the Fourth Lateran Council recognized, God does not judge criminal guilt, at least not for us. After blessing us with reason and the power to choose, God may have given us responsibility for other awesome decisions as well—choices that we would rather leave to God but cannot.

We speak of rationing resources and think of scarcity. Our new responsibility for choice has arisen, however, not because the resource of life has grown rarer but because it has grown more plentiful. A gift for which we can only be grateful has brought with it a new obligation to confront a very old issue.

7

CONCLUSION

For many, the emerging public debate about active voluntary euthanasia may be seen not only as a serious breach of a social taboo but also as one more vicious attack on the value of human life. Their response will likely be framed in the language of the right to life. For others, it may be considered the culmination of efforts to achieve ever greater autonomy over one's life. Their response to the debate will likely be framed in the language of the right to die. The battle lines will be drawn—the right to life vs. the right to die—and as a society we will have missed a rare opportunity for a richer, deeper, more fruitful debate.

We hope that this guide has given a sense of the complexity of the issue and of the ambiguity accompanying any position. The issue is not as simple as being for or against active voluntary euthanasia; nor can the debate be reduced to the right to life vs. the right to die, negative consequences vs. positive consequences, slippery slope arguments vs. their rejection. These elements undoubtedly have their place in the discussion. Yet to remain focused on them is to ignore deeper issues.

Some of these issues have been alluded to in these pages. For example, we currently care for the dying with a highly technological, cure-oriented medicine. The fears and difficulties generated by this approach are surely real and need to be reckoned with. But it would be short-sighted at best to opt for direct termination of life before we have made a serious attempt to change the factors contributing to a desire for euthanasia. The troubling aspects of current attitudes and practices involved in the care of the dying should not be left intact because of too quick a move toward euthanasia.

There are yet other issues to be addressed—more profound and more elusive. They may be clustered under the umbrella of core beliefs. Individuals hold convictions about human nature, about the ultimate purposes of life, and about the meaning of pain, suffering, finitude, dependency, and death. These beliefs shape how they perceive and experience illness, healing, dying, and other fundamental human realities. Whether suffering, for example, is seen as an unmitigated evil to be eliminated in any way possible, or as punishment, or as formative of the self, or as somehow redemptive will depend to a considerable degree on one's view of human existence itself. Is it to pursue pleasure and avoid pain, or to strive toward self-realization, or to achieve union with a transcendent reality? How one answers this question (and there are many ways) will influence one's view of death. It may be seen as an absurd annihilation of all human experience and achievement, or as the culmination of one's lifelong process of self-creation, or as deliverance from this earthly journey, or passage to a destiny beyond life. The debate about active voluntary euthanasia, if it is not rushed and narrowed to a debate about rights and consequences, could provide an opportunity for lifting up and reexamining a host of relevant core beliefs.

Religious traditions have a crucial role to play in this connection. Seeking the meaning of the most fundamental of human experiences brings one, after all, to the threshhold of the religious, and the religious traditions have a long and rich history of interpreting these realities. But not all interpretations are adequate or can speak to a secular, technological culture. The euthanasia debate, in fact, challenges religious traditions to examine and perhaps reinterpret or reformulate their accepted understandings. They may need to take another look at their long-standing arguments against suicide and active euthanasia. What *is* the moral evil in active euthanasia? Is it really identical to the evil that we condemn in other forms of terminating life? Is ending the life of a terminally ill person always incompatible with responsible stewardship of the gift of life received from the

Creator? These and other questions deserve a fresh look marked by openness and honesty.

Finally, perhaps it is time for us as a society to come to terms with the notion of autonomy particularly as it bears upon public policy. What is at issue here is the relation of the individual to the community. An increasing chorus of voices in recent years has been calling into question the sacrosanct status given to the autonomy of the individual in the United States. These critics perceive the problem as lying not so much with autonomy as with its scope, its limits, and its frequent neglect of responsibilities to other individuals, to society as a whole, and to the common good. The language of rights needs to be complemented with the language of responsibilities. Probing the appropriateness and the wisdom of a public policy regarding active voluntary euthanasia could provide space for a much needed debate about a major underlying presupposition of our society.

The emerging controversy about the justifiability and social acceptability of active voluntary euthanasia provides individuals, communities, and society with a singular opportunity for addressing constructively and creatively some of the most fundamental issues we can face. We would do well to be careful about the framing of the debate and certainly cautious about any hasty resolutions.

Ron P. Hamel

NOTES

Chapter 2: A Brief Historical Perspective

1. For historical surveys of euthanasia, see Paul Carrick, *Medical Ethics in Antiquity* (Dordrecht: D. Reidel, 1985); Gerald Gruman, "Death and Dying: Euthanasia and Sustaining Life: Historical Perspectives," *Encyclopedia of Bioethics*, ed. William Reich (New York: Free Press, 1978), 261–68; W. Bruce Fye, "Active Euthanasia: An Historical Survey of Its Conceptual Origins and Introduction into Medical Thought," *Bulletin of the History of Medicine* 52 (Winter 1978), 492–502.

2. According to *The Oxford English Dictionary*, the term *euthanasia* was first used in 1646.

3. Carrick, *Medical Ethics in Antiquity*, 127.

4. If euthanasia was involuntary (that is, against the patient's will and wishes), the relevant moral category was homicide, according to the Greeks. When speaking of active voluntary euthanasia, where the patient chooses to carry out euthanasia through the agency of another, suicide was considered an appropriate and applicable category. Robert N. Wennberg, *Terminal Choices: Euthanasia, Suicide, and the Right to Die* (Grand Rapids, Mich.: Eerdmans, 1989), 16. Wennberg notes that *suicide* in contemporary use is not a neutrally descriptive term but carries a strong negative connotation. In part, this connotation reflects the censure of suicide by the religious traditions which have heavily influenced postclassical Western culture. Interestingly, however, the term *suicide* was introduced into English in 1651 by Walter Charleton to make available a more neutral and less judgmental term for acts of self-killing, which had come to be viewed as "murdering oneself"—a phrase that conveys firm disapproval. This word did not exist in Latin but was an invention achieved by combining two Latin words, *sui* (self) and *cide* (kill). No longer the neutral term it was intended to be, negative attitudes toward self-killing have become attached to the word (p. 18).

5. At least eight recurring types of suicide that were recognized during the Greco-Roman period. See A. W. Mair, "Suicide," *Encyclopedia of Religion and Ethics*, ed. James Hastings (New York: Scribner's, 1966), 12: 26–33.

6. Carrick, *Medical Ethics in Antiquity*, 261. This type of suicide, which we may call voluntary euthanasia, is illustrated by the elderly citizens of Ceos who, once they had passed age 60, were in the habit of taking leave from life by drinking hemlock. See Jerry B. Wilson, *Death by Decision: The Medical, Moral, and Legal Dilemmas of Euthanasia* (Philadelphia: Westminster Press, 1975), 20; also cited in Carrick, 133. For an interesting discussion of classical attitudes toward suicide, see Danielle Gourevitch, "Suicide Among the Sick in Classical Antiquity," *Bulletin of the History of Medicine* 43 (1969): 501–18.

7. Carrick, *Medical Ethics in Antiquity,* 136.

8. *Phaedo* 62 b–c, trans. Hugh Tredennick, *The Collected Dialogues of Plato,* ed. Huntington Cairns and Edith Hamilton (New York: Random House, 1966), 45.

9. *Republic* 3.407d, trans. Francis Cornford (Oxford: Oxford University Press, 1973), 97.

10. *Nichomachean Ethics* 3.1116a. 12–15, trans. W. D. Ross, *The Basic Works of Aristotle,* ed. Richard McKeon (New York: Random House, 1941), 977.

11. Carrick, *Medical Ethics in Antiquity,* 144–148. For Seneca's view on the need for active euthanasia, see Derek Humphry and Ann Wickett, *The Right to Die: Understanding Euthanasia* (New York: Harper and Row, 1986), 5.

12. Carrick, *Medical Ethics in Antiquity,* 149–50. See also the discussion of the Stoics in Wennberg, *Terminal Choices,* 42–45.

13. Plato, cited in Humphry and Wickett, *Right to Die,* 4; Plato, *Republic,* trans. B. Jowett (New York: D. Van Nostrand, 1959), 297.

14. "The Hippocratic Oath," trans. Ludwig Edelstein, in *Selected Papers of Ludwig Edelstein,* ed. Lilian C. Temkin and Owsei Temkin (Baltimore: Johns Hopkins University Press), 6.

15. See Carrick, *Medical Ethics in Antiquity,* 81–87, 6–18; see also Gourevitch, "Suicide." 501–518.

16. Carrick, *Medical Ethics in Antiquity,* 81.

17. Humphry and Wickett, *Right to Die,* 6.

18. A. Alvarez, *The Savage God: A Study of Suicide* (New York: Bantam Books, 1976), 68.

19. Darrel W. Amundsen and Gary B. Ferngren, "Medicine and Religion: Early Christianity Through the Middle Ages," in *Health/Medicine and the Faith Traditions,* ed. Martin E. Marty and Kenneth L. Vaux (Philadelphia: Fortress Press, 1982), 94–95.

20. Gruman, "Death and Dying," p. 261.

21. Interestingly, there is little evidence of any contact between Hippocratic medicine and Christianity prior to the ninth century. The growing injunction against euthanasia rested on religious grounds rather than the Greek medical tradition. Robert Veatch and Carol Mason, "Hippocratic Versus Judeo-Christian Medical Ethics: Principles in Conflict," *Journal of Religious Ethics* 15 (Spring 1987): 86–105.

22. Thomas Aquinas, *The Summa Theologica of St. Thomas Aquinas* 2.2 Q. 64, a.5, trans. Fathers of the Dominican Province (London: Burns, Oates, and Washbourne, 1929), 10:202–5.

23. Sir Thomas More, *Utopia,* from *The Complete Works of St. Thomas More,* ed. Edward Surtz and J. H. Hexter (New Haven: Yale University Press, 1963), 4: 186.

24. Michael MacDonald, "The Medicalization of Suicide in England: Laymen, Physicians, and Cultural Change, 1500–1870," *Millbank Quarterly* 67 (Supplement 1, 1989): 74.

25. For a discussion of Bacon's views on euthanasia as an "essential area of medical skill," see Gruman, "Death and Dying," 262.

    During the sixteenth and seventeenth centuries, Catholic moral theologians began to make use of a distinction between direct and indirect killing in discussions about prolonging, as well as terminating, the life of a dying patient. The distinction was originally found in Aquinas's treatment of self-defense and hinged on the notion of *praeter intentionem* (not directly intended). Richard A. McCormick, "Principle of Double Effect," *The Westminster Dictionary of Christian Ethics*, ed. James F. Childress and John Macquarrie (Philadelphia: Westminster Press, 1986), 162. Given the Christian view of life as a divine gift, one could never directly intend the death of an innocent. "However, if one's direct deed and intention are focused on a defensible human good (e.g., self-defense), then the indirect result (the aggressor's death) is regrettably accepted, though unintended, and the agent is morally free of blame." Richard C. Sparks, *To Treat or Not to Treat?* (New York: Paulist Press, 1988), 91. These considerations had implications for medical care. While the distinction disallowed active euthanasia, it did permit the cessation of physicians' efforts to prolong patients' lives when treatments were of little or no benefit or were excessively burdensome and there was no intention to kill.

26. See Fye, "Active Euthanasia," 497–99.

27. Gruman, "Death and Dying," 264.

28. See Gruman, "Death and Dying," 265–66.

29. Walter Cane, "Marx's 'Medical Euthanasia,' " *Journal of the History of Medicine* 7 (1952): 413; cited in Fye, "Active Euthanasia," 495.

30. Fye, "Active Euthanasia," 496–497. The term *euthanasia* was first used in this sense in 1869 by British intellectual historian W. E. H. Lecky; see Wennberg, *Terminal Choices*, 4.

    With the development of effective analgesics in the nineteenth century, the earlier distinction in Roman Catholic theology between direct and indirect killing came to be applied to the administering of pain-killing drugs that sometimes led to patients' deaths. Catholic moral theologians resolved this dilemma with the principle of double effect. Actions involving both good and evil effects were said to be justifiable if four conditions held: (1) the action from which the evil effect results itself was good or indifferent; (2) the good effect and not the evil effect was the one sincerely intended by the agent; (3) the good effect was not produced by means of the evil effect; and (4) there was a proportionately grave reason for allowing the foreseen evil effect to occur. When these conditions are fulfilled, the resultant evil is referred to as an "unintended by-product" of the action, justified by the presence of a proportionately grave reason. McCormick, "Principle of Double Effect," 162. Therefore, a dose of analgesia that led to a patient's death could be considered morally permissible if the patient's pain was so grave as to require it and if the drug was administered with the proper therapeutic intention. The patient's death was an unintended by-product of the therapeutic intention, i.e., to relieve pain.

31. Samuel D. Williams, "Euthanasia," in *Essays of the Birmingham Liberal Club* (Birmingham, 1870); see the discussion of this essay in Fye, "Active Euthanasia," 498.

32. Fye, "Active Euthanasia," 501.

33. See, for instance, James Rachels, "Active and Passive Euthanasia," *New England Journal of Medicine* 292 (9 January 1975): 75–80; David C. Thomasma and Glenn C. Graber, *Euthanasia: Toward an Ethical Social Policy* (New York: Continuum, 1990), 66–80. Also see R. D. Mackey, "Terminating Life-sustaining Treatment—Recent U. S. Developments," *Journal of Medical Ethics* 14 (September 1988): 135–39. For a thorough discussion of recent legal considerations regarding euthanasia, see Sandra Segal Ikuta, "Dying at the Right Time: A Critical Legal Theory Approach to Timing-of-Death Issues," *Issues in Law and Medicine* 5 (1989): 3–66.

Chapter 4: Views of the Major Faith Traditions

1. Sources for these descriptions are Constant H. Jacquet, Jr., ed., *Yearbook of American and Canadian Churches 1988* (Nashville: Abingdon Press, 1988); Frank S. Mead, with a revision by Samuel S. Hill, *Handbook of Denominations in the United States*, 8th ed. (Nashville: Abingdon Press, 1985); J. Gordon Melton, *The Encyclopedia of American Religions*, 2 vols. (Wilmington, N.C.: McGrath Publishing, 1978); Ronald L. Numbers and Darrel W. Amundsen, eds., *Caring and Curing: Health and Medicine in the Western Religious Traditions* (New York: Macmillan 1986); and relevant volumes in the Park Ridge Center's Health/Medicine and the Faith Traditions series published by Crossroad.

2. Elliot N. Dorff, "The Jewish Tradition," in *Caring and Curing*, ed. Numbers and Amundsen, 7–8.

3. Dorf, "The Jewish Tradition," 7.

4. Fred Rosner, "The Jewish Attitude Toward Euthanasia," in *Jewish Bioethics*, by Fred Rosner J. and David Bleich (Brooklyn, N.Y.: Hebrew Publishing, 1979), 260.

5. Quoted from Rosner, "The Jewish Attitude Toward Euthanasia," 261.

6. Quoted from Rosner, "The Jewish Attitude Toward Euthanasia," 261.

7. Quoted from Rosner, "The Jewish Attitude Toward Euthanasia," 262.

8. Immanuel Jakobovits, *Jewish Medical Ethics*, (New York: Bloch Publishing, 1975), 123–24.

9. Walter Jacob et al., Responsa 79, "Euthanasia," *American Reform Responsa* (1980).

10. David M. Feldman and Fred Rosner, eds., *Compendium on Medical Ethics;* 6th ed. (New York: Federation of Jewish Philanthropies of New York, 1984), 106.

    For a discussion of euthanasia by representatives of Conservative Judaism see Barry D. Cytron and Earl Schwartz, *When Life Is in the Balance: Life and Death Decisions in Light of the Jewish Tradition* (New York: Youth Commission, United Synagogue of America, 1986). We drew on many of the Jewish sources cited in their discussion.

    For a dissenting voice in Conservative Judaism, see David M. Shohet, "Mercy Death in Jewish Law," *Conservative Judaism* 8 (April 1952): 1–15.

11. Fazlur Rahman, "Islam and Health/Medicine: A Historical Perspective," in *Healing and Restoring: Health and Medicine in the World's Religious Traditions*, ed. Lawrence E. Sullivan (New York: Macmillan, 1989), 150.

12. First International Conference on Islamic Medicine, *Islamic Code of Medical Ethics*, Kuwait Document, Kuwait Rabi 1, 1401 (January 1981).

13. Quoted in Gerald A. Larue, *Euthanasia and Religion: A Survey of the Attitudes of World Religions to the Right-to-Die* (Los Angeles: Hemlock Society, 1985), 110.

14. Quoted in Larue, *Euthanasia and Religion*, 108.

15. Christian Life Commission Board, *Policy and Procedures Manual of the Christian Life Commission of the Southern Baptist Church* (1987), 3. This position is reaffirmed in "Christian Life Commission Staff Guidelines for the Publishing of Materials on Abortion and Euthanasia," revised version (September 1988), no. 4.

16. Social Issues Commission of the General Association of General Baptists, *The Social Principles of General Baptists* (Poplar Bluff, Mo.: General Report of General Baptists, 1989), 9.

17. D. Duane Cummins, *A Handbook for Today's Disciples* (St. Louis, 1981), 46–47.

18. Cummins, *Handbook*, 45.

19. Larue, *Euthanasia and Religion*, 114–15.

20. This tradition is contained in Anglican moral theology and discussions of the Council for Health and Human Values and the House of Bishops as well as in research and discussions of the Episcopal Board for Social Responsibility.

21. Larue, *Euthanasia and Religion*, 116. This material was taken from "Mercy Killing," *Awake!* 8 May 1978, 28.

22. Larue, *Euthanasia and Religion*, 117. This material was drawn from "Mercy Killing," *Awake!* 8 March 1978, 7.

23. Communication received from Church Headquarters of the Church of Jesus Christ and the Latter-day Saints, Salt Lake City, Utah, 11 July 1990. This statement reflects the policy contained in *The General Handbook of Instruction of the Church of Jesus Christ of Latter-day Saints* (1989), which is published for leaders of the church at the general and local levels. The *Handbook* has the approval of the First Presidency.

24. Communication of 11 July 1990.

25. Resolution 3–30, "To Affirm Sacredness of Human Life," Lutheran Church–Missouri Synod, *1977 Convention Proceedings*, 138.

26. Lutheran Church–Missouri Synod, Commission on Theology and Church Relations, Social Concerns Committee, *Report on Euthanasia with Guiding Principles* (October 1979), 7.

27. American Lutheran Church, Office of Research and Analysis, Task Force on Ethical Issues in Human Medicine, "Death and Dying" (July 1977), 3.

28. Larue, *Euthanasia and Religion*, 91.

29. Larue, *Euthanasia and Religion*, 87.

30. Larue, *Euthanasia and Religion*, 78–81. This was originally published in *Church and Society* 73, no. 6 (July/August 1983).

31. Larue, *Euthanasia and Religion*, 82.

32. General Assembly of Unitarian Universalists, *1988 Proceedings*, 74.

33. Stanley S. Harakas, as quoted in Larue, *Euthanasia and Religion*, 54.

34. Harakas, as quoted in Larue, *Euthanasia and Religion*, 54.

35. Stanley S. Harakas, *Contemporary Moral Issues* (Minneapolis: Light and Life Publications, 1982) 171.

36. Harakas, *Contemporary Moral Issues*, 174–75.

37. Harakas, *Contemporary Moral Issues*, 176.

38. Harakas, *Contemporary Moral Issues*, 172–73. Harakas also discusses active euthanasia in his book *Health and Medicine in the Eastern Orthodox Tradition* (New York: Crossroad, 1990), 157, and in "Eastern Orthodox Christianity," *Encyclopedia of Bioethics* (New York: Free Press, 1978), 1:351–52.

39. Larue, *Euthanasia and Religion*, 56–57.

40. See Prakash N. Desai, "Medical Ethics in India," *Journal of Medicine and Philosophy* 13 (August 1988): 231–55.

41. Prakash N. Desai, *Health and Medicine in the Hindu Tradition* (New York: Crossroad, 1989), 18–21.

42. Desai, *Health and Medicine*, 93–97.

43. T. Gyatso, *The Opening of the Wisdom Eye* (Wheaton, Ill.: Theosophical Publishing House, 1974), 53–64.

44. Pinit Ratankal, "Bioethics in Thailand: The Struggle for Buddhist Solutions," *Journal of Medicine and Philosophy* 13 (August 1988): 301–12.

45. S. Gyatso, *Essence of Refined Gold*, trans. and ed., G.H. Mullin (Ithaca, N.Y.: Gabriel/Snow Lion, 1982), 87–88.

46. Larue, *Euthanasia and Religion*, 136–37.

47. Phillip A. Lesco, "Euthanasia: A Buddhist Perspective," *Journal of Religion and Health* 25 (Spring 1986): 55.

Chapter 5: Is Active Euthanasia Justifiable?

Reflection: Ronald E. Cranford

1. S. H. Wanzer et al., "The Physician's Responsibility toward Hopelessly Ill Patients: A Second Look," *New England Journal of Medicine* 320, no. 13 (30 March 1989): 844–49.

2. W. Gaylin et al., "Doctors Must Not Kill," *Journal of the American Medical Association* 259, no. 14 (1988): 2139–40.

Reflection: James F. Bresnahan

1. S. H. Wanzer et al., "The Physician's Responsibility toward Hopelessly Ill Patients: A Second Look," *New England Journal of Medicine* 320, no. 13 (30 March 1989): 844–49.

2. Compare the discussion in Wanzer et al., note 1, with Wanzer et al., "The Physician's Responsibility toward Hopelessly Ill Patients," *New England Journal of Medicine* 310, no. 15 (12 April 1984): 955–59.

3. See Bulkin and Lukashok, "Rx for Dying: The Case for Hospice," *New England Journal of Medicine* 318, no. 6 (11 February 1988): 376–78.

4. C. K. Cassel and D. E. Meier, "Sounding Board: Morals and Moralism in the Debate over Euthanasia and Assisted Suicide," *New England Journal of Medicine* 323, no. 11 (13 September 1990): 750–52.

5. See Leon R. Kass, "Mortality and Morality: The Virtues of Finitude," chap. 12 of *Toward a More Natural Science: Biology and Human Affairs* (New York: Free Press, 1985), 299–317.

Reflection: Karen Lebacqz

1. See Stanley Hauerwas, "My Uncle Charlie May Not Be Much of a Person but He's Still My Uncle Charlie," in *Truthfulness and Tragedy* (Notre Dame, Ind.: Notre Dame University Press, 1977).

2. Nel Noddings, *Caring: A Feminine Approach to Ethics and Moral Education* (Berkeley and Los Angeles: University of California Press, 1984), 32: "The mother as one-caring ... wants first and most importantly to relieve her child's suffering."

3. How much misogyny entered that decision is beyond the scope of this piece.

FOR FURTHER READING

Books

Brody, Baruch. *Suicide and Euthanasia*. Hingham, Mass.: Kluwer, 1989.

Feldman, David M., and Fred Rosner, eds. *Compendium on Medical Ethics: Jewish Moral, Ethical and Religious Principles in Medical Practice*. New York: Federation of Jewish Philanthropies of New York, 1984.

Grisez, Germain, and Joseph M. Boyle, Jr. *Life and Death with Liberty and Justice*. Notre Dame, Ind.: University of Notre Dame Press, 1979.

Gula, Richard. *What Are They Saying About Euthanasia?* Mahwah, N.J.: Paulist Press, 1986.

Horan, Dennis J., and David Mall, eds. *Death, Dying, and Euthanasia*. Frederick, Md.: University Publications of America, 1980.

Humphry, Derek, and Ann Wickett. *The Right to Die: Understanding Euthanasia*. New York: Harper and Row, 1986.

Kohl, Marvin, ed. *Beneficent Euthanasia*. Buffalo, N.Y.: Prometheus Books, 1975.

Kuhse, Helga. *The Sanctity-of-Life Doctrine in Medicine: A Critique*. Oxford: Oxford University Press, 1987.

Larue, Gerald. *Euthanasia and Religion: A Survey of the Attitudes of the World Religions to the Right-to-Die*. Los Angeles: Hemlock Society, 1985.

Maguire, Daniel. *Death by Choice*. New York: Schocken Books, 1975.

McCarthy, Donald G., and Albert S. Moraczewski. *Moral Responsibility in Prolonging Life Decisions*. St. Louis, Mo.: Pope John XXIII Medical-Moral and Research Center, 1981.

Rachels, James. *The End of Life: Euthanasia and Morality*. New York: Oxford University Press, 1986.

Thomasma, David, and Glenn C. Graber. *Euthanasia: Toward an Ethical Social Policy*. New York: Continuum, 1990.

Veatch, Robert. *Death, Dying, and the Biological Revolution*. Rev. ed. New Haven and London: Yale University Press, 1988.

Vere, Duncan W. *Should Christians Support Voluntary Euthanasia?* London: Christian Medical Fellowship, 1971.

———. *Voluntary Euthanasia: Is There an Alternative?* London: Christian Medical Fellowship, 1971.

Wennberg, Robert N. *Terminal Choices: Euthanasia, Suicide, and the Right to Die*. Grand Rapids, Mich.: Wm. B. Eerdmans, 1989.

Theological Articles

Cahill, Lisa S. "A 'Natural Law' Reconsideration of Euthanasia." *Linacre Quarterly* 44 (February 1977): 47–63.

Desai, Prakash. *"Karma,* Death, and Madness." Chap. 8 of *Health and Medicine in the Hindu Tradition: Continuity and Cohesion*. New York: Crossroad, 1989.

Fletcher, Joseph. "The Right to Live and the Right to Die: A Protestant View of Euthanasia." *Humanist* 34, no. 4 (July/August 1974): 12–15.

Furlong, Francis P. "Conflicting Protestant Views on Euthanasia." *Linacre Quarterly* 18 (November 1951): 91–98.

Goldman, Alex J. "Euthanasia." In *Judaism Confronts Contemporary Issues*, 171–91. New York: Shengold Publishers, 1978.

Gula, Richard. "Euthanasia: A Catholic Perspective." *Health Progress* 68, no. 10 (December 1987): 28–31.

———. "Moral Principles Shaping Public Policy on Euthanasia." *Second Opinion* 14 (1990): 72–83.

Hauerwas, Stanley, and Richard Bondi. "Memory, Community and the Reasons for Living: Theological and Ethical Reflections on Suicide and Euthanasia." In *Truthfulness and Tragedy*, 101–15. Notre Dame, Ind.: University of Notre Dame Press, 1977.

Klein, Isaac. "Euthanasia: A Jewish View." In *Perspectives on Jews and Judaism*, ed. Arthur A. Chiel, 249–55. New York: Rabbinical Assembly, 1978.

Lesco, P. A. "Euthanasia: A Buddhist Perspective." *Journal of Religion and Health* 25, no. 1 (1986): 51–57.

Maguire, Daniel C. "The Freedom to Die." *Commonweal* 96 (11 August 1972): 423–27.

May, William E. "Euthanasia, Benemortasia, and the Dying." *Linacre Quarterly* 41 (May 1974): 114–23.

McCormick, Richard A. "The Consistent Ethic of Life: Is There an Historical Soft Underbelly?" In *Consistent Ethic of Life*, 96–122. Kansas City: Sheed and Ward, 1988.

Meilaender, Gilbert. "Euthanasia and Christian Vision." *Thought* 57 (December 1982): 465–75.

Minogue, Brendan P. "The Exclusion of Theology from Public Policy: The Case of Euthanasia." *Second Opinion* 14 (1990): 84–93.

Nelson, Robert J. "Euthanasia: A Dilemma for Christians." *Engage/Social Action* 13 (April 1985): 32–40.

Novak, David. "Euthanasia in Jewish Law." In *Law and Theology in Judaism*, 98–117. New York: Ktav Publishing House, 1976.

Overduin, Daniel C. "Euthanasia." *Lutheran Theological Journal* 14 (December 1980): 114–23.

Rahman, Fazlur. "Passages: Death." In *Health and Medicine in the Islamic Tradition*. 125–29, New York: Crossroad, 1987.

Ramsey, Paul. "Euthanasia and Dying Well Enough." *Linacre Quarterly* 44 (February 1977): 37–46.

Riga, Peter. "Euthanasia." *Linacre Quarterly* 41 (February 1974): 55–65.

Rosner, Fred. "Jewish Attitude Toward Euthanasia." In *Modern Medicine and Jewish Law*, 107–23. New York: Yeshiva University, 1972.

Simmons, Paul D. "Euthanasia: The Person and Death." In *Birth and Death: Bioethical Decision Making*, 107–54. Philadelphia: Westminster, 1983.

Nontheological Articles

Admiraal, Pieter V. "Justifiable Euthanasia." *Issues in Law and Medicine* 3 (Spring 1988): 361–70.

Bostrom, Barry. Euthanasia in the Netherlands: A Model for the United States? *Issues in Law and Medicine* 4 (July 1989): 467–86.

Callahan, Daniel. "Vital Distinctions, Mortal Questions." *Commonweal* (15 July 1988): 397–404.

Campbell, Courtney, and Bette-Jane Crigger, eds. "Mercy, Murder, and Morality: Perspectives on Euthanasia." *Hastings Center Report* 19 (January/February 1989): 1–32.

Cassel, C. K., and D. E. Meier. "Morals and Moralism in the Debate over Euthanasia and Assisted Suicide." *New England Journal of Medicine* 323 (13 September 1990): 750–52.

Conolly, Matthew E. "Alternative to Euthanasia: Pain Management." *Issues in Law and Medicine* 4 (July 1989): 497–507.

Davies, Jean. "Raping and Making Love Are Different Concepts: So Are Killing and Voluntary Euthanasia." *Journal of Medical Ethics* 14 (1988): 148–49.

Dessaur, C. L. and C. J. C. Rutenfrans. "The Present-Day Practice of Euthanasia." *Issues in Law and Medicine* 3 (Spring 1988): 399–405.

Devettere, Raymond J. "Reconceptualizing the Euthanasia Debate." *Law, Medicine, and Health Care* 17 (Summer 1989): 145–55.

Driesse, Marian H. N., et al. "Euthanasia and the Law in the Netherlands." *Issues in Law and Medicine* 3 (Spring 1988): 385–97.

Gaylin, Willard, et al. "Doctors Must Not Kill." *Journal of the American Medical Association* 259, no. 14 (8 April 1988): 2139–40.

Gert, Bernard, and Charles Culver. "Distinguishing between Active and Passive Euthanasia." *Clinics in Geriatric Medicine* 2 (February 1986): 29–36.

Graber, Glenn. "The Rationality of Suicide." In *Suicide and Euthanasia: The Rights of Personhood,* ed. Samuel E. Wallace and Alben Eser, 51–65. Knoxville: University of Tennessee Press, 1981.

Jonsen, Albert. "Beyond the Physician's Reference—The Ethics of Active Euthanasia." *Western Journal of Medicine* 149 (August 1988): 195–98.

FOR FURTHER READING

Kass, Leon. "Death with Dignity and the Sanctity of Life." *Commentary* (March 1990): 33–43.

Lundberg, George. "'It's Over, Debbie' and the Euthanasia Debate." *Journal of the American Medical Association* 259 (8 April 1988): 2142-43.

Mayo, David. "The Concept of Rational Suicide." *Journal of Medicine and Philosophy* 11 (May 1986): 143–55.

Montague, Phillip. The Morality of Active and Passive Euthanasia. *Ethics in Science and Medicine* 5 (1978): 39–45.

Rachels, James. Active and Passive Euthanasia. *New England Journal of Medicine* 292 (1975): 78–80.

Robertson, John. Euthanasia: The Collision of Theory and Practice. *Law, Medicine, and Health Care* 18, nos. 1–2 (Spring/Summer 1990): 105–7.

Rosenblum, V. G., and C. D. Forsythe. The Right to Assisted Suicide: Protection of Autonomy or an Open Door to Social Killing? *Issues in Law and Medicine* 6, no. 1 (Summer 1990): 3–32.

Segers, J. H. "Elderly Persons on the Subject of Euthanasia." *Issues in Law and Medicine* 3 (Spring 1988): 407–24.

Shaffer, Catherine. Criminal Liability for Assisting Suicide. *Columbia Law Review* 86 (March 1986): 348–76.

Singer, Peter. "Euthanasia—A Critique." *New England Journal of Medicine* 322, no. 26 (28 June 1990): 1881–83.

van der Sluis, I. "The Practice of Euthanasia in the Netherlands." *Issues in Law and Medicine* 4 (July 1989): 455–65.

Vaux, Kenneth. "Debbie's Dying: Mercy Killing and the Good Death." *Journal of the American Medical Association* 259 (8 April 1988): 2140–41.

Weinfeld, D. J. "Active Voluntary Euthanasia—Should It Be Legalized?" *Medicine and Law* 4 (1985): 101–11.

Wolhandler, S. "Voluntary Active Euthanasia for the Terminally Ill and the Constitutional Right to Privacy." *Cornell Law Review* 69 (1984): 363–83.